The Grand Finale

A Quilter's Guide to Finishing Projects

by Linda Denner

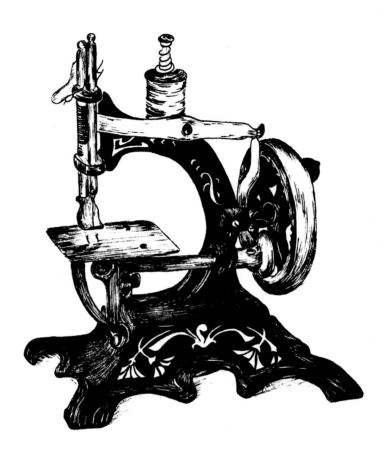

On the Cover

Duck pillow with knife edge finish, Fish and Ships wallhanging with diagonal set, neckroll pillow, and antique Pinetree Variation quilt top displayed on trunk. All designs save the antique quilt originals by Author.

The Grand Finale

A Quilter's Guide to Finishing Projects

by Linda Denner

American Quilter's Society

P.O. Box 3290 • Paducah, Kentucky 42001

Dedication

For Len, who has shared my life, all my dreams
and goals. Through your dedication and artistry with
a camera, this book has become a reality.

Pineapple Sorbet wallhanging, Unicorn skirt, quilter's tote bag, ruffled pillow and Double Wedding Ring quilt all by Author.

Acknowledgment

There are many influences in our lives, but my sewing and quilting direction was navigated by two patient and loving women, Grace Krause and Bobbie Brannin. "Aunt Grace" took the time to teach an enthusiastic and persistant child of eight how to sew. Years later, my first quilting teacher, Bobbie Brannin, opened my life to patchwork and has remained a beloved friend ever since.

Credit

Photographs by Len Denner

Illustrations and Drawings by Pamela C. Denner

Antique child's sewing machine, small cabinet, various sewing impliments owned by Author.

Table of Contents

An Introduction

This is not a pattern book, nor a book that takes the quilter through the step by step construction of a specific project. This is a photographic journey through the steps of completing pillows, quilts, and wallhangings. Zippers, ruffles, piping, mitering, continuous bias are presented from the sewer's vantage point. Following our step by step photographs should carry your project out of its storage box and to its proper setting in your home.

Today most people come to quilting without a good working knowledge of sewing. The sewing that they have experienced was limited to six weeks in junior high school, where they usually hated it. Once assured that dressmaking has nothing to do with quilting, the new quilter jumps in with enthusiasm. Their fervor does tend to wear thin however, when the final moments of completion draw near. Aside from the common fear of leaving hundreds of yards of untouched fabric to our surviving kin, the next greatest fear of quilters is to leave a chest or closet of unfinished projects. With our image in jeopardy as accomplished Needle Artists, we must set about completing our work from time to time. Hopefully with the use of this text you can finish them all and perhaps have a bit more fire for the end of a project.

I will not give a list of supplies, for I assume that in order to have worked upon your project up to the point of completion you have utilized needle, thread and assorted equipment. As the photographs display tools that I have found most helpful I will make note of their availability.

Feel free to use this book in the order in which you need the information contained. Information is given independently within each chapter.

With a little adjustment, I am certain that the experienced sewer will also be able to incorporate some of these techniques into her standard bag of tricks. Above all, approach your work with humor and an open mind. Remember, if one method is not successful for you, try another. Work when you feel fresh and do not push yourself when battling fatigue. Many techniques simply cannot be clearly shown with illustrations, and if you have experienced difficulty following a method in the past we hope that through our photos you will, at last, see their merit.

We have all made resolutions to finish all our projects before starting something new. This text should help you in this effort, and demonstrate that the finale of the project offers excitement and design potential to the very end.

Chapter One — Pillows

Pillows.

The first and most common use for our pieced and appliqued blocks is in the construction of pillows. Nothing can make a room more personalized than the accent touch of pillows. They make welcome presents for our friends and give us the opportunity of exploring new patterns and colors without the commitment of a large quilt. Portable and fun to make, never make excuses for being a pillow maniac. Just make sure you finish what you start. Explore a variety of styles creating a change of pace for your eye when grouping pillows together. Some styles of finish can immediately render a pillow feminine or masculine in appearance. It goes without saying that a beautifully finished pillow treatment can raise a simple preprinted panel to a very special gift.

Let us initially deal with the issue of filling for pillows. Your options range from stuffing your pillow with shredded rubber, polyfill, used nylon stockings or pillow forms. Which is best? What do I use and where do you get it? Experience is naturally the greatest teacher, but I hope to share some practical information acquired over the years for your benefit.

If the pillow you are making is a standard size, usually an even number like 10″, 12″, 14″ and so forth, a form will be available for your use. Forms wear best and retain their shapes with hard use. I do purchase the size that is closest in size to the pillow front. The manufacturers have allowed room to ease their product into its prescribed space.

It would be ideal if quilters made pillows all in predictable and even shapes. Reality is indeed very different. We make blocks because they are fun and often

have no idea what to do with them when they are finished. All too often we decide that the 17″ Mariner's Compass would make a wonderful Father's Day present for Dad. Don't be surprised if you create a charming scene for a pillow front that is 12″ x 18″. Pillow form manufacturers cannot anticipate our creative sizing and we must find alternate methods of stuffing our pillows. Stuffing the pillows with polyfill is the next and easiest answer. Using old stockings is an alternate but they can result in a lumpy finish. You should naturally wash the nylons and cut off the toes and elastic tops before use. I do not use stockings myself as I would rather fill my limited storage space with fabric, thread, patterns and books on quilting. With space at a premium, I am selective about my compulsions.

If you find yourself in the position of filling an odd size pillow, you can make a suitable pillow form by using polyester batting and polyfill. Select a stiff polyester batting for the task. Cut the batting the finished size you require, and sew around the outside with a ¼″ seam. It will not be necessary to reverse this so you may use a zigzag stitch along the edges. Fill the pocket through an open side and complete stitching up your opening. This type form will prevent the polyfill from lumping when you launder.

It is important to point out at this time that manufacturers of polyfill make a variety of grades of polyfill. The best grade is processed more thoroughly and has a minimum amount of threads and small lumps. This product will have a fluffier quality and will therefore require less fill to complete the stuffing of your pillow. The initial cost of the package will be greater; however, the product will go further thus being more cost effective.

Utilizing down for a filling is another option. Down is the most expensive filling. You would need to construct a muslin pillow casing slightly smaller than the finished pillow size. Fill this muslin form with the down. Five years ago a friend of mine acquired a large amount of down. She made me a 14″ muslin pillow form of the material for a sample. I covered the form with a patchwork design for my living room and placed it on our sofa. My family has proceeded to treat this pillow with the lack of respect they evenhandedly treat all my pillows. It has been thrown on the floor, across the room, slept upon and leaned upon. It is today in the same condition as the day I first placed it on the couch. I am amazed at its durability. If this filling is available to you, I could not recommend it more.

Shredded rubber is another method of filling your pillow cavity. This is by far the most difficult product to use for stuffing. The rubber generates so much static electricity that the only feasible place to stuff will be out of doors. This is the least expensive product available for this purpose. The hidden cost will be your time as it will require some effort to handle the material and smooth out the small ridges created by the rubber chunks.

With the many options available for filling, you should suit the purpose of the pillow to the method employed to stuff it. You should find all the fillings discussed in this text available through your local fabric and notions stores. With holiday pillow treatments I prefer to close with a zipper or envelope closure. This allows me to store the designs flat when not in use, and slip a more year round design onto a common pillow form. When presenting pillows for gifts, I usually omit the zipper closure and use a form or stuffing to finish off. I am content that the recipient will be able to properly launder the gift; I will save myself the time and the expense of the zipper.

Pillow for a holiday gift.

Assembling and Trimming Pillows

The beauty of patchwork and quilting is that it is enjoyable to those of us who are not experienced with a sewing machine. When it comes to assembling the project, the sewing machine is the tool to use. Great proficiency on the machine is not necessary. It will not be necessary to own an expensive and elaborate model sewing machine. Check to see that your machine is in proper running condition. And more importantly when completing pillows check the size of the needle you will be using in the machine. Many quilters feel that they are wise in keeping costs low by maintaining the same machine needle year after year. There are no rewards in heaven for she who possesses the oldest machine needle. When the needle is dull, you will not have the proper tension or service from your machine. When the size of the needle is too small, the machine will labor to sew through the thicknesses. It is a good rule of thumb that upon com-

pletion of every sewing project, treat your machine and yourself to a new needle. In most cases, to stitch through a pillow front, batting, ruffle and pillow backing, your machine will operate efficiently with a size 14 needle. Since most patchwork is with woven material, it will not be necessary to use ballpoint needles.

When sewing on batting, you will generate a large amount of lint in your machine bobbin. Please check your manual and clean your machine frequently.

Making Continuous Bias Binding

For use in making piping, trimming a pillow that is circular, or binding the edge of clothing or quilts, the most useful process to master is making your own bias binding. My favorite method is commonly referred to as "Continuous Bias." This process creates a tube of fabric that will be later cut into one long strip of continuous bias binding. I believe that this is the most difficult process to illustrate due to its three dimentional nature. Our photos will hopefully solve this dilemma. Additionally, most references start the sewer off using a 36″ square of cloth. This will indeed yield enough bias to trim two quilts. The most useful results of this method, however, is that with a small amount of fabric the process will yield a usable amount of bias for many needs. To calculate the amount of bias your square will yield, measure the square across the diagonal from one corner to its opposite corner. Divide this diagonal measurement in half, and take this number and divide this once more by the width of the strips you will be cutting. This figure will tell you how many strips of a given width you will yield. Each strip will be the length of the side of the square. For example, if your square is 18″ in size, the diagonal will be 25″. Half of this figure is 12½″. Cutting strips 1½″ wide will yield approximately 10 strips that are 18″ long. With a yield of 10 strips you will have five yards of bias from an 18″ square. As you can readily see, an 18″ square will bind the edge of most standard sized baby quilts or bind the edge of four placemats. This is one case where a little will yield a lot. This process is a "Must" in your bag of tricks.

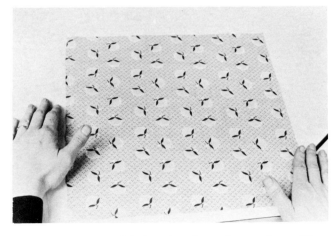

Cut a square of fabric, trimming selvage edges off.

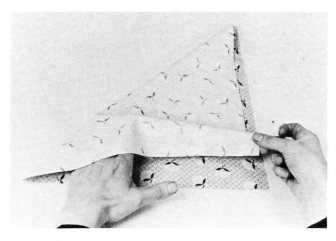

Bring diagonally opposite corners together and fold diagonally.

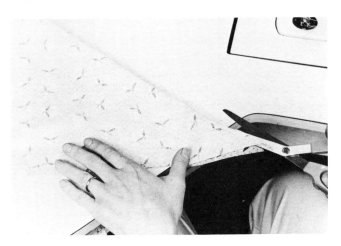

Cut along the diagonal fold line.

You should now have two separate triangle sections.

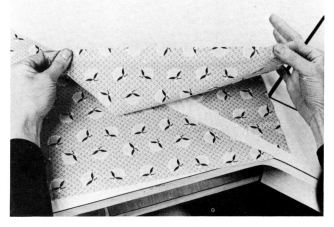

It will be necessary to reassemble these two sections into a tube by sewing similar grained sides together. To enable you to determine the grain of the short sides of the triangles after trimming the selvage off, pull slightly along their outside edges. One of the short sides will stretch gently as you pull, while the other short side will not stretch at all. The two sides that do not stretch are the lengthwise grain of the fabric.

Position the two lengthwise grain sides with their right sides facing each other, and pin the sides evenly in place.

Sew with ¼″ seam allowance along the pinned side using 12 to 15 stitches to the inch.

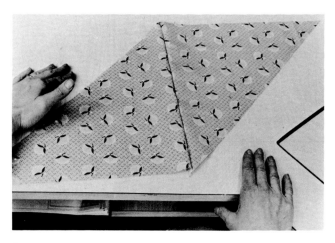

Open the sewn section. It should resemble a parallelogram as the photo suggests.

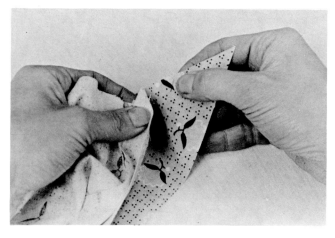

Place the lower right corner even with the marked line.

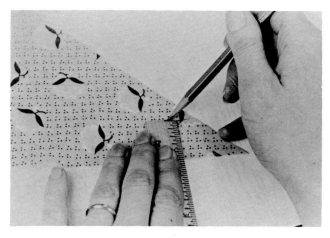

From the upper right corner on the right side of your fabric, mark into the top edge the width of the bias you wish to cut. If you are using a standard 1½″ bias make a mark using a ruler 1½″ over.

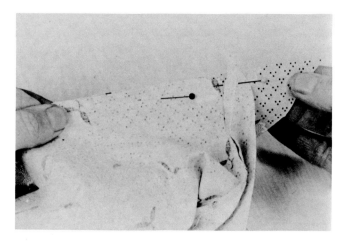

Position the two edges even with each other, and pin the two sides a shown.

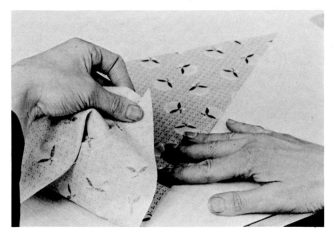

Place your hand on the lower right hand corner, and with a twisting motion bring this corner up to the upper right hand corner.

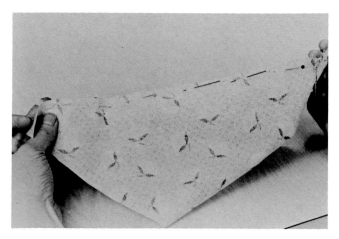

Pin along the length of this edge.

After pinning, the unit should form a tube as the photo indicates.

Sew along the pinned edge with ¼″ seam allowance.

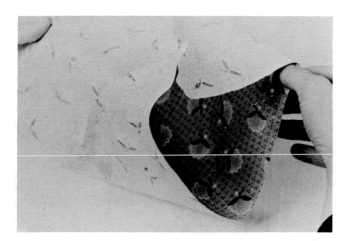

When sewing is complete, your triangles should form a tube.

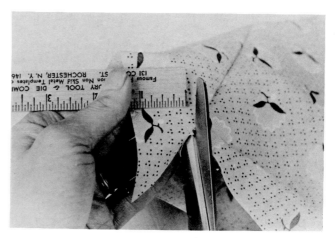

When you sewed the second seam, you began by offsetting the edges the width of the bias to be cut. You should now have extentions that are 1½″ beyond the sides of this seam. With a small ruler in hand, measure for a length of perhaps 6″ from the outside edge 1½″. Cut this section 1½″ wide.

Fold this band back over the tube and use this as a guide to cut the entire tube into a uniform width.

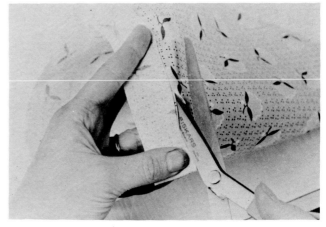

Be careful to cut one thickness at a time. Sliding the tube over the narrow edge of an ironing board may help you to cut without fear of clipping into several layers at a time.

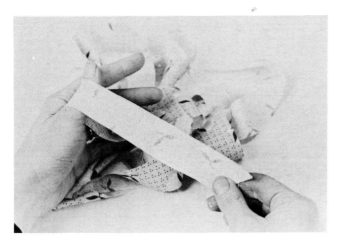

This method will provide adequate lengths of evenly cut bias for all your quilting needs.

Rainbow Bias

For a new and unusual effect in bias trimming, try making your bias from assorted strips of calico.

Cut 6 strips of calico across the grain of your fabric each 3½" x 42".

Now proceed to make your bias tube in the same manner as shown before. The bias should have the correct stretch if you have cut and sewn your strips in the same grain direction. When the bias is cut, you will have a delightful rainbow effect. This will add a great accent to a plain muslin square and be just the perfect compliment to a baby quilt made in the primary colors. In addition to being a colorful treatment, this is another trick to use when you have only scraps of calico left at the end of a project, and you may find the fabric you used no longer available.

With your bias made, you are prepared to use it for a variety of chores.

Trimming Pillows with Piping

Making your own piping for the edging of a pillow will be our first consideration. You may purchase cording at local fabric stores in a choice of weights. The heaviest weights are intended for upholstering furniture and the medium to light weights are for piping on pillows or clothing. You can purchase this by the yard. Use the zipper foot attachment for your sewing machine. Position the foot as close as possible to the cord while placing your bias over the cord. The bias should be placed with the right sides out. Sew with 10 to 12 stitches per inch using a matching colored thread to place the cord in the center of the bias strip. Sew the cording within the entire run of bias in the length that you require for your project.

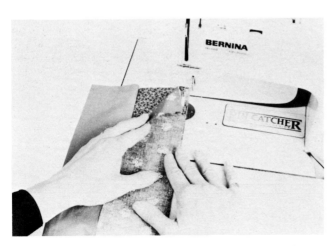

Piece these together along their 42" lengths and press.

If you are using commercially available piping, look carefully along the stitching line of the piping. There is indeed a right and a wrong side of the piping. This can readily be determined by the stitching on the piping. The right side has a finished stitch, and the wrong side is slightly more pronounced. Prepare to attach the cording by placing an easily recognized colored thread in the bobbin of your machine. The purpose for this will be shown in the pillow assembly. Always trim the batting and muslin layer for quilting even with the top edges of your pillow before starting.

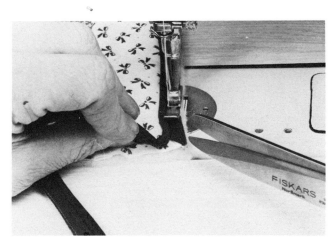

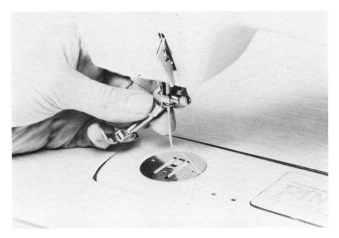

Place the zipper foot on your sewing machine. The zipper foot works best to attach piping, allowing you to sew directly on the piping seamline. You will find that the top layer you are working with, in this case the piping, will be pushed faster by your machine than the underlayer of the pillow front. Extensive pinning may make you feel secure, but in this case it will be counterproductive. If you pin, you will need to remove all the pins as you work when the piping shifts during sewing. If you have trimmed your edges and allowed ¼″ seam allowance along your edge, use the stitching line of the piping to guide your work.

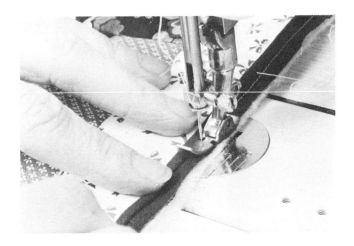

Hold the edges firmly together and sew without pins. Sew the seam even with your pillow edge using ¼″ seam and a stitch length of 10 stitches to the inch.

About two inches before you approach the corner of the pillow, approximate where the corner will meet the piping. Cut into the piping up to the stitching line on the piping at this point. Sew up to the clipped point on this side. Leaving the needle in the fabric at the corner point, lift your pressure foot and rotate the pillow one quarter turn until the next side is in line with the edge of your presser foot. Release the pressure foot and continue to attach the remaining three sides in the same manner.

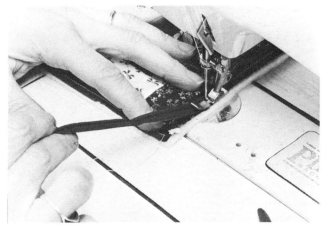

Cross the piping over the beginning section when you have completed all four sides. For average weight piping, this will provide an inconspicuous ending. When your cording is thick, or you have a circular edge to the pillow, you will want to attach the ends of your bias into a continuous band. Cut the piping ends allowing ½″ each for seam allowance. Overcast the cording firmly together. Seam the ends of the bias together with an inside seam, and continue to attach it all around the edges of your shape.

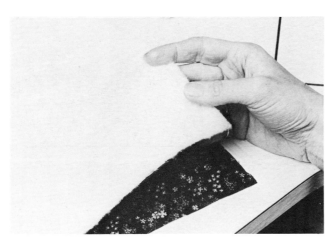

If you have placed a dark thread in the bobbin of your sewing machine, you can now easily see your sewing line on the wrong side of the pillow front. Place the pillow front over the backing.

Using the stitching line that you used to connect your piping, follow this to stitch the pillow front to the back.

Clip across the corners as shown before reversing.

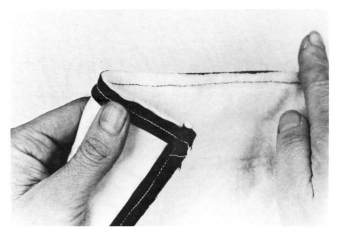

The dark bobbin stitching line can be your guide whenever you sew trimming to the front of your pillows.

Trimming with Preshirred Ruffling

The next method we can use to trim the edge of a pillow is using a preruffled trimming.

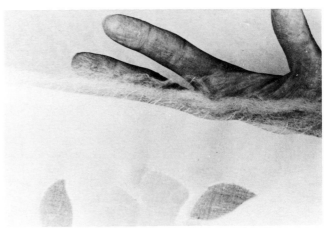

In all cases, it will be easier for you to assemble your pillow by cutting the edge of the batting and muslin behind the pillow top, even with the top edges. You can then use the edge as a sewing guide.

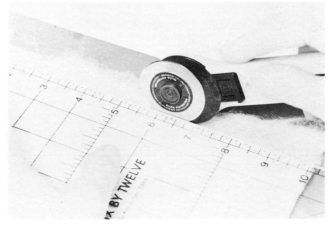

Rotary cutters have so many applications in patchwork today. Use this tool here to cut an even edge when cutting multiple layers.

The raw edges should be even as shown.

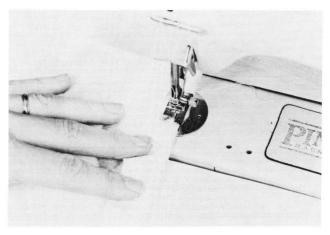

Sew in the stitching line of the binding as this will provide a standard ¼″ seam.

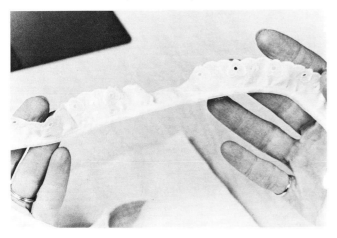

Eyelet trim, like piping has a right and wrong side that is distinguished by the stitching on the binding. The wrong side will have a chain stitch, and this is the side facing you when positioning the trim.

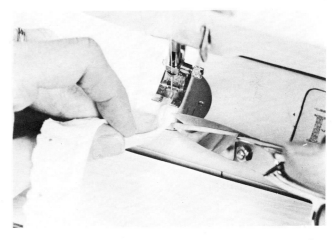

When you reach a corner of the pillow, approach the edge and stop ¼″ from the corner. Fold in a small tuck of the ruffling in the corner to add fullness in this area when the pillow is reversed. Keep your needle in the work, and raise the pressure foot of your machine.

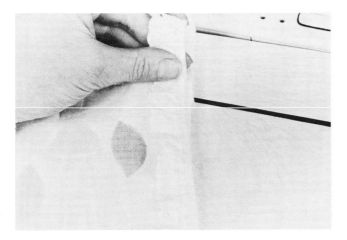

Start attaching the trim in the center of one side of the pillow front.

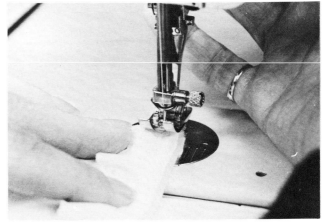

Pivot the pillow until the next side is even with the sewing line of the machine. Release the pressure foot to its downward position and continue to sew along the new side.

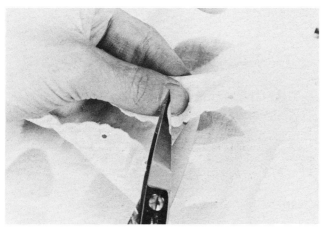

When you have completed all the sides of the pillow and are approaching the beginning of the trim, you should prepare to stop. Refrain from sewing at least two inches from where the ends will meet.

Sew them with the wrong sides coming together and a ¼" seam as shown. Remove the work from the machine.

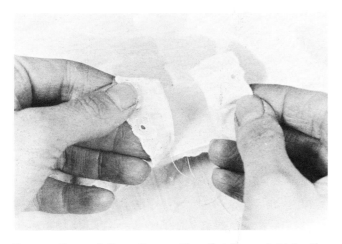

Remove the work from the machine. Cut the eyelet trim the finished length you will need plus ½" for seam allowance.

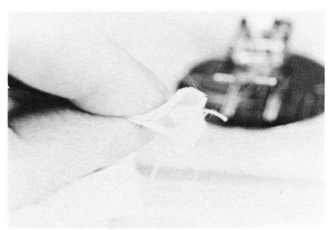

Flip this seam in on itself.

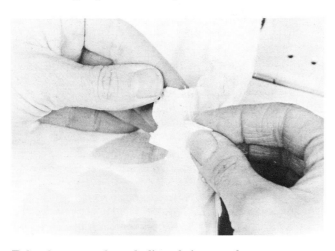

Take the two ends and align their raw edges.

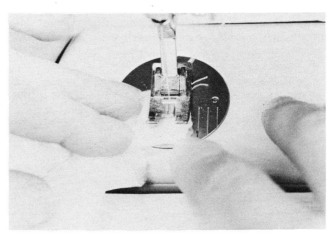

Sew with a ¼" seam as shown to encase the raw edges. This is a machine sewn french seam that will give a tidy appearance and a strong finish when joining trim. Once the ends have been attached, complete the seaming of the trim to the pillow side. As in the case of attaching piping, the trimming line is more visible if you keep a different colored thread in the bobbin of the machine.

Ruffles

Ruffles are the most popular and attractive finishes for the edges of pillows. They can add size to a small pillow front and make a beautiful statement in your decorating. There are several methods of ruffling, and I will show each, and let you decide which one you will use as the need arises. As I am a miser with my fabric, I only use bias for ruffling when I trim a circular edge. In the case of a round or heart shaped hoop or pillow, I bite the bullet and use bias. The bias will create a ruffle that will round curved edges. However, it uses a far greater amount of fabric. When I am making a simple ruffle for a square or rectangular pillow, I use fabric that has been cut on the cross grain of the material. This allows me to use as little as a half yard for a ruffle up to the size of a 12″ pillow. The ruffle is very nice, and I can live to use my premium calico for another day.

Make a long basting stitch by machine sewing along the raw edge within the outer ¼″ of this band. This will prevent the raw edges from shifting as you proceed to ruffle the material.

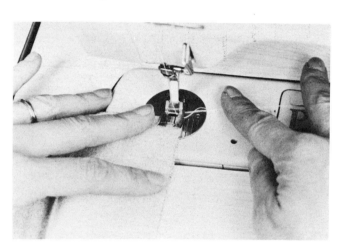

Let us start by making a ruffle for a 12″ square pillow. It is often suggested that to have sufficient fullness you double or triple the perimeter of the surface you are trimming. In actual practice, I have found this is too much bulk to work with and an overwhelming amount of fabric to sew into a pillow. I use a convenient amount cut with my rotary cutter across the grain of the fabric. In the case of a 3″ ruffle, I cut two strips of fabric 6″ wide by the width of the material, 42″. This amount will be adequate for any pillow up to 12″ square. I start by sewing the two 6″ lengths together to form a band of 84″.

Iron the fabric with the right sides out creasing the center line. This should now give you a band 3″ x 42″ with right sides turned outwards.

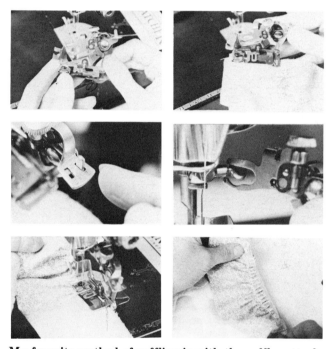

My favorite method of ruffling is with the ruffler attachment for my sewing machine. This attachment is so under-utilized and can save many hours of work. Years ago this attachment was included with the purchase price of most machines. It is indeed intimidating, with so many levers and screws, but lets have a careful look at the contraption. All rufflers have two places of attachment to the machine. One is the normal foot attachment spot, and an opened circular hook that must be placed round the needle screw. With use, you will find the screw vibrates the needle loose, so be sure to check this from time to time. The front of the attachment has a lever as indicated in the photo that has a series of numbers and a star. The numbers indicate the amount of fullness your ruffler is gathering, and when you move the lever to the star, the ruffler stops ruffling altogether. Stopping the ruffler in the midst of your work allows you to attach additional material if you need it without removing this somewhat clumsy foot. Stopping the ruffling further permits you to gather a section, have an ungathered space, then resume your ruffling when you desire. The fabric that you wish to ruffle is placed between the two pieces of blue steel on the foot. When you have positioned your material correctly, it will resist being pulled back, because it will be held by the blades of blue steel. Whatever you place completely under the attachment will be stitched but not ruffled. This means that with a little practice you may gather your ruffles and sew it to the edge of a curtain, for example, all in one operation. What a clever little foot! The big question, of course, is how much does your ruffler ruffle? Take a sample scrap of fabric, let's say 10″. Gather this in the ruffler and measure it when it is sewn. Repeat this for each setting, and you will be able to judge how much fabric you require for each job. I use the medium setting for all ruffling jobs, and it gathers about 1½ its length in fullness. This is slightly more generous than commercially manufactured trimming.

When turning the corner, pivot by lifting your pressure foot again and keep your needle down in the fabric. Turn and resume your stitching.

When I attach a ruffle to the pillow edge, I start attaching the ruffle in the middle of one side of the pillow, just as I do in the case of attaching eyelet trim.

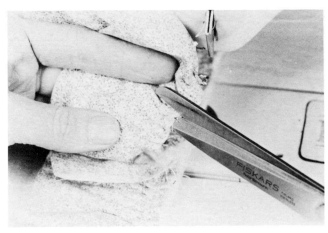

When you have returned to the starting position, trim the edges of the ruffle adding at least ¾″ extra for both ends. Your edges should be unattached to the pillow top.

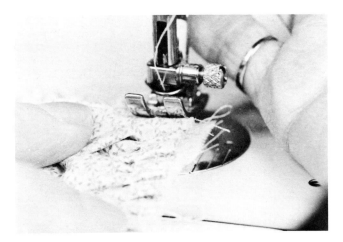

You will have to fold additional fullness in the corners. Folding a small box pleat in the corners should give you ample fullness when you reverse the pillow right sides out.

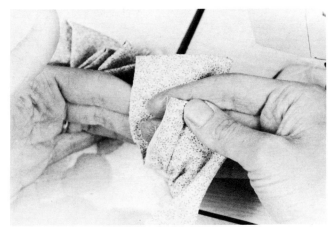

Flip the edges with the wrong sides facing in.

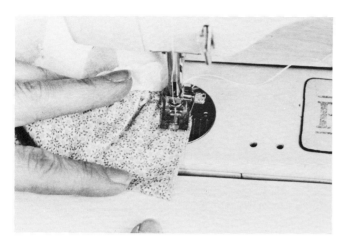

Sew with ¼″ seam allowance.

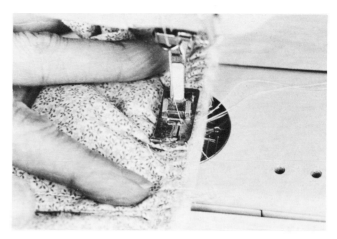

Continue to machine sew this final amount to the pillow front.

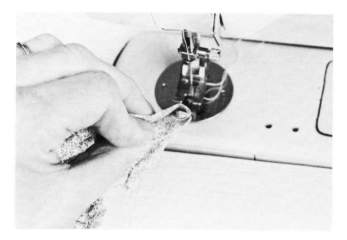

Fold the right sides of the fabric over this seam.

The most common error in attaching a pillow front and back is catching the ruffle in the seam as you stitch. This makes a short project into a long frustating evening. I take great pains to avoid bloopers like this. Fold the ruffle into the corners away from the seams, and secure this with a strip of masking tape. If you fear catching the center side of the ruffle as well, add tape here also. A little tape goes a long way to improve the job and your disposition.

Stitch along the folded seam. This will enclose the first seam forming a french seam.

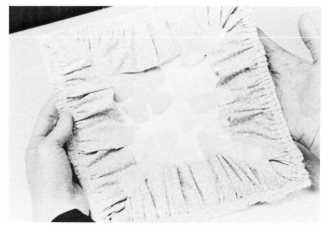

The prepared front should have all corners taped flat.

Now it is time to sew the pillow front to the back. If you have used foresight, you put a clearly visible colored thread in your bobbin when attaching the ruffle. If not, you are now appreciating the value of such a step. Lay the back of the pillow on a flat surface, and place the front with right sides over the back, facing down. Be sure your side edges are even on the front and back, and pin the pillow together.

Now reverse. Remove the tape.

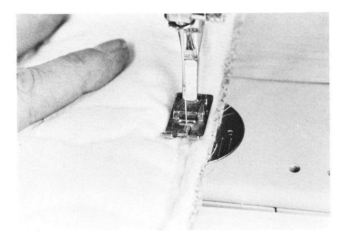

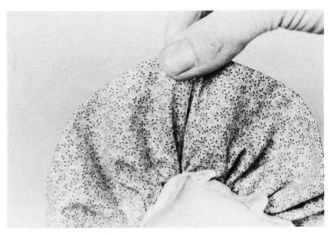

Gently pull the corners out.

Sew with ¼″ seam allowance. If you are using a pillow form, and no zipper, plan on leaving one side completely open. If you are using polyfill to stuff the pillow, complete the four corners, and leave an adequate space in the center of one side to allow your hand to fit in the opening without fear of tearing your fabric.

Stuff with small amounts of polyfill at a time.

Before reversing your pillow, you must cut across the corners diagonally. The corner will not reverse properly if you are timid about this cut. If you are insecure and fear the corner stitching will come out, you can reinforce this with two lines of stitching.

When stuffing, fill the corners first, making them firm to the touch. Work your way out, and remember that with wear the stuffing will settle.

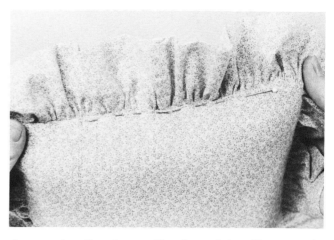

As you pin, align the outside edges of the pillow to maintain smooth side.

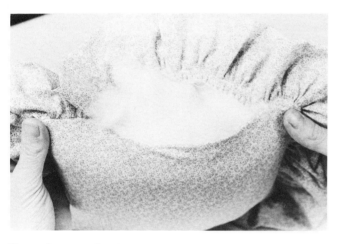

Turn the raw edge in.

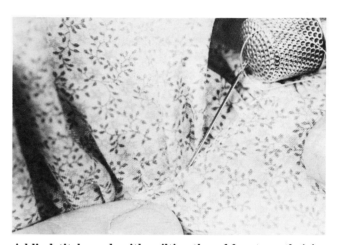

A blindstitch, made with quilting thread for strength, joins the fold of your seam allowance with the stitching line of the ruffle seam.

Pin the back edges over the front at the ruffle attachment seam.

Your pillow is now ready to add special charm to your room.

There are times that a ruffler attachment may not be available to you, or this procedure may not fit your needs.

Gathering with Parallel Threads

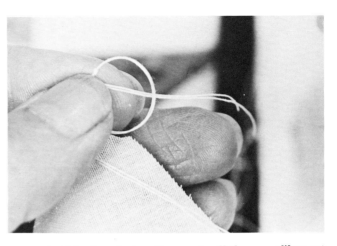

Tie the bobbin threads together, and pull the monofilament gently.

The most common method taught to gather fabric is to sew two parallel rows of machine basting stitches. If you use nylon monofilament thread in the top of your sewing machine for this procedure, you will find the thread breakage is eliminated and the fabric will slide on the thread more readily.

Do not sew one row of stitches when gathering. You will not achieve an even fullness, and you stand a greater risk of thread breakage.

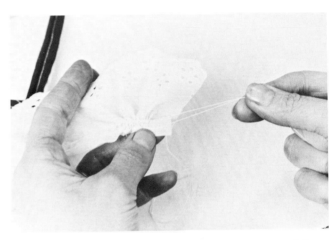

Separate the bobbin and top sewing threads.

Remember if you are gathering a long band of material you should be pulling from both ends. This shares the stress of the fabric on your threads evenly.

Gathering with Zig Zag Stitches

Sewing is like all other facets of life, and there are many ways to skin a cat and gather a ruffle as well. If your sewing machine does a zig zag stitch, you can gather the heaviest fabric in a foolproof manner demonstrated below.

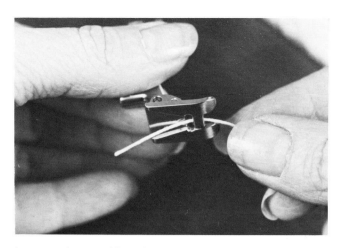

Some sewing machines feature a presser foot with a small hole in its lower part. This is to insert a cord for various purposes during sewing.

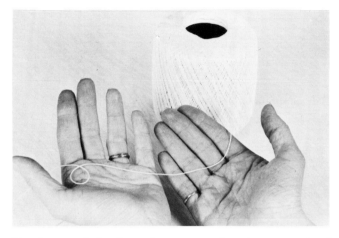

Purchase a skein of pearl cotton or gimp from your local variety or craft store. Measure this cord to the finished size you require and add an additional 6″ for knots and your peace of mind.

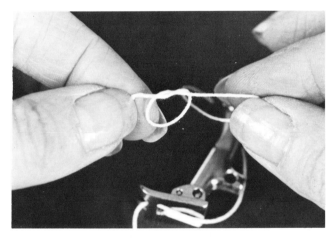

Insert the pearl cotton into this opening if you have such a foot. If you are using a general purpose foot, lay the cording in the center of this foot.

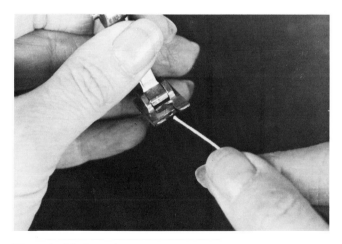

Tie a double knot in the end of the cord, and position the cord in the center of your general purpose sewing foot.

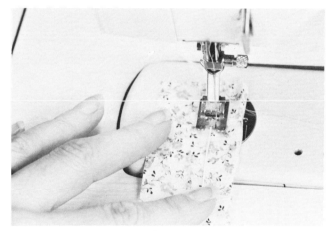

Set your machine to a wide zig zag with a long stitch length of about 8 stitches to the inch. The knot should be toward the back of the machine. Zig zag over the cord. As you sew, you should hold the cord tightly as the photo suggests, gathering the fabric evenly as you sew. Let the cord run the length of the fabric to be ruffled. Remove the ruffle from the machine and knot the other end of the cord to eliminate it from pulling out of the zig zag stitching. You can now adjust the fullness of the ruffle and position it in place with pins.

The cord is strong, so you may gather a dust ruffle for a bed without fear of the gathering threads breaking. After you have sewn the ruffle down, if you have avoided sewing the cord, you can cut the knot, and remove the cord from your work.

Multi-Strip Ruffles

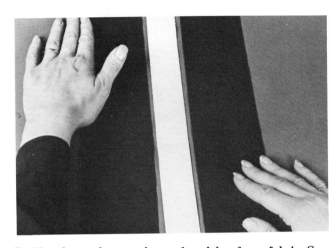

Ruffles do not have to be made solely of one fabric. Sew strips of multiple widths of fabric together to create variety in your ruffles. If you want two fabrics combining to make the ruffle, cut them with the grains going in the same direction to eliminate puckering their seams. Remember, they will collectively add up to the size you need, and you must add seam allowance for their assembly. The ruffle shown in the photo will total 6″ as in our earlier example. I want a narrow band of color on the outside edge, and I am therefore cutting this band from two lengths of 42″ wide callico, and 1½″ in width. From the second calico cut four strips 2½″ x 42″ long.

Sew the bands together first, to make each section 84″ long. Position the 1½″ strip between the two 2½″ bands. Sew these along their 84″ long. Position the 1½″ strip between the 2½″ bands. Sew these along their 84″ sides. Press the seams to one side. Press the assembled band in half, with the right sides out as in the case of a solid ruffle previously discussed.

You will see a ½″ band of color on both sides of this ruffle. I prefer not to work with a band narrower than a finished one inch. Irregularities in your sewing are more obvious with smaller strips.

Knife Edged Pillows

Knife edge pillow treatments are a great option for finishing a pillow. They use little fabric or trimming to complete, little time, and a small amount of polyfill. I think that they offer a contemporary treatment suitable for modern decors and can be ideal for a masculine look. The pillow front in the photo was a small block that I had made experimenting with Joyce Schlotzhauer's Curved Two Patch System. It resulted in a small 6″ square that was very attractive but of little use without making many more for a wallhanging or quilt.

Place the zipper foot on your sewing machine. You must sew in the ditch of the panel/band seam around the three sides of the panel parallel to the sewn pillow edges. Leave the same panel side open as the outer edge. Your stitching should be as inconspicuous as possible when sewing this seam. I would recommend using a matching colored thread, or nylon monofilament in the top thread of your machine. Use sewing thread in the bobbin to match the back of your pillow. The zipper foot will allow you to sew as close as possible to the seamline.

With a pillow in mind, I cut borders of 2½″ and surrounded the block with this strip. Since the block unit was only 2″, a wider border would have overwhelmed the square. I had made this block several years before and had long past used most of the fabrics that were in the design. With some luck, I could extend the scraps I did have by adding 2½″ squares in the four corners. (This technique is shown in the chapter on finishing your quilt). It is important, as in the case of framing a block in a knife edge pillow, to have batting behind the bands as well as the patchwork panel. The bands may also be made from a heavy weight fabric like corduroy or upholstery material.

Fill the inner cavity of your pillow with polyfill.

Cut a pillow back the same finished size as the top of your pillow. Sew the back and front together, leaving one side completely open as the photo shows. Clip your corners diagonally, and reverse the pillow. Press the pillow edges flat.

Pin the fourth side of this panel closed when it is completely stuffed.

Machine sew the last side closed.

Attach two bands for forming the pillow ends.

Hand sew the outer edge of the pillow to complete the pillow.

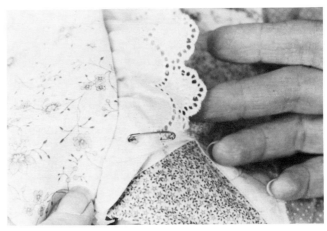

Pin trimming out of your way.

Neckroll Pillows

The last style pillow you may need to finish is a neckroll pillow. This is made from a rectangular or square shape of fabric.

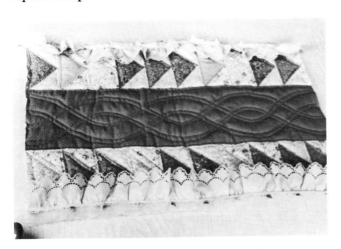

Attach trimming to either side of the pillow front.

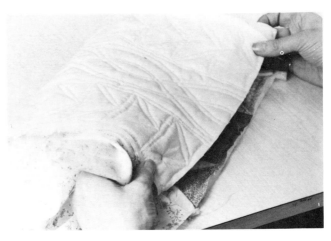

Bring the two long sides together and pin.

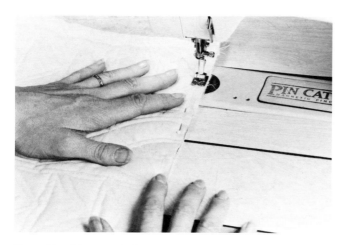

Sew this side with ¼" seam allowance.

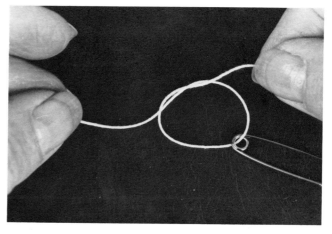

Attach the ribbon or string to the end of a safety pin.

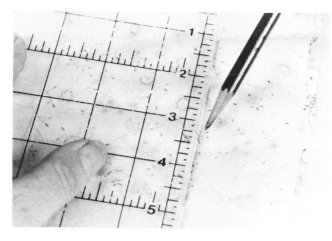

Trim the panels the side width of half the diameter measurement of the rounded pillow ends. Add 1" to this measurement for a casing.

Run the ribbon through the casing.

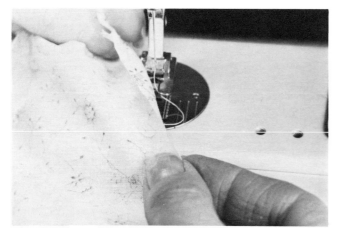

Sew a narrow casing by folding a ½" hem of fabric along the outside edge of the bands. Leave a small opening along your casing edge for inserting a string or ribbon.

Pull the ribbon tightly, drawing the band together to close one side of the pillow.

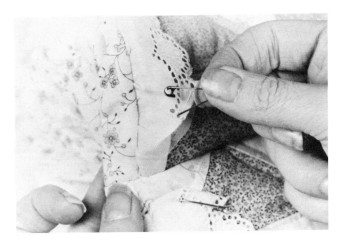

Unpin the eyelet and trim it adding seam allowance.

Insert a ribbon in the open side and draw this ribbon into a bow for trim, or tie a secure knot if you are planning to conceal the side construction.

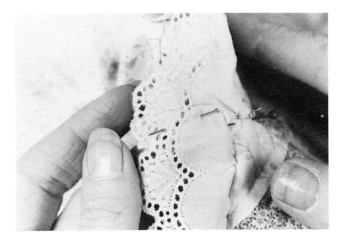

Sew the ends of the eyelet together by hand.

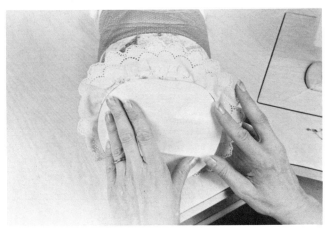

Using a simple compass draw a circle the size of the ends using your diameter size as a guide.

Insert a roll of battling cut the same length as your pillow.

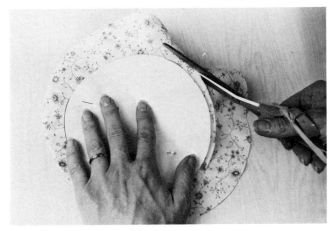

Add a ¼″ seam allowance to this pattern and cut two circles from your fabric.

Baste back the seam allowance around the circumference of the circles.

The circle will cover the opening and drawn ends of the pillow.

Pin the circle to the edge of the pillow ends.

If you wish to show the gathering on the side, cover a button with a circle of fabric, and sew this in the side center as an alternate finish.

Hand applique the circles to either end of the pillow to complete the project, and conceal the side gathering.

Inserting a Zipper

Sooner or later non-sewing quilters will wish they knew the correct technique to insert a zipper into a seam. If you can match the seams of a nine patch you can stitch in a little zipper, but let me make some suggestions beforehand. Zipper manufacturers, like our pillow form manufacturers, cannot keep up with the sizing we quilters need to complete our projects. Did you know you can cut down any zipper to accommodate your need once it is sewn into a seam? Fabric stores frequently reduce the prices of their long zippers, and I might add, seldom have the shorter skirt lengths at reduced prices. I keep a supply of various colors that I pick up on sale ranging in size from 18″ to 22″. At times I have been lucky to purchase these at five for one dollar. After I sew these into the seam I need, I cut the excess ends away. Your seams will act as the stop on the zipper. Naturally you must sew the zipper in closed.

You have the choice of location of the zipper completely at your discretion. If someone enters your home, sits on your couch and comments on the incorrect placement of the zippers on your pillows, simply do not ask them back as a guest to your home. Zippers can be positioned in the center back of the pillow or on the side of the pillow. Given the choice, take the center back. This is much easier to manipulate.

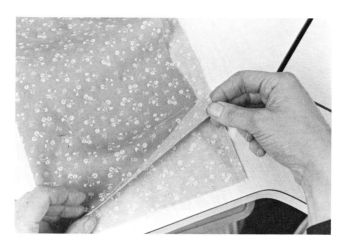

I would work with a piece of fabric 15″ x 12½″.

Fold this piece in half, and cut it into two 7½″ sections.

If the pillow front is 12½″ as an example, you will need a larger piece of backing fabric than this measurement.

A zipper seam must be at least ½″, and the additional width for the backing is half the front and a bit extra for peace of mind. Sew these two pieces together along the 7½″ length with a machine or hand sewn basting stitch.

Iron the seam open.

Look carefully at the zipper you are going to use. The manufacturers have anticipated our needs and woven a clear ridge on the wrong side of all zippers indicating where you should stitch. Center the teeth of the zipper, wrong side up on the pressed seam. Pin this in place, and baste the zipper, if you like, in place to prevent shifting.

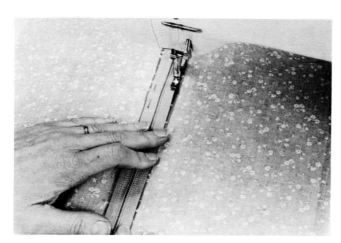

Place the zipper foot on your sewing machine, and sew along one side on the woven ridge with a 12″ to 15″ stitch length.

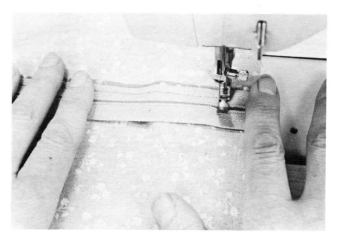

When you reach the bottom of one side and need to cross over the remaining side, pivot your needle by keeping the needle down and raising the presser foot. Realign the stitch line parallel to the lower edge and hand turn the wheel of your machine to cross the teeth of the zipper. If you machine sew this quickly at a normal speed, you may hit the zipper teeth and break the needle. Breaking the needle will cause no permanent damage to your machine, but it is inconvenient in the middle of a procedure and annoying.

When you have completed your stitching, remove your work from the machine. Cut the excess zipper length, if you have any.

Remove the basting stitches from your seam.

Center the pillow front over the pillow back, and trim the back to fit the patchwork front.

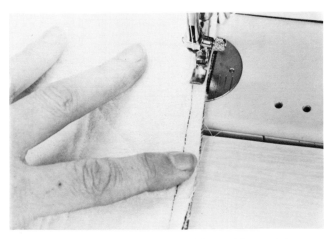

If you have trimmed your front with a ruffle or piping, you should have a clear stitching line to follow when sewing the back and front together. Lay the pillow back on a flat surface, and position the front, right sides facing each other, over the back. Remember to trim all batting and muslin from the front to an edge even with the trimming. Pin the layers firmly together. Sew the edge around all four sides. Your zipper should be closed for this procedure.

Once the stitching is completed, with a little manipulation you should be able to pull the tab of the zipper down, and open the zipper completely. The zipper opening will provide the place to reverse your pillow.

Before reversing, remember to *cut the corners diagonally* to insure sharp pillow corners. Insert the pillow form.

The alternate location for inserting a zipper is in one of the side seams of the pillow. If you have used a patchwork or quilted backing for the pillow, thus making it reversible, you would naturally not want to insert a zipper in the center back. For zipper side insertion the steps are as follows:

1. Baste the seam that you wish the zipper to be inserted in together. This will join the pillow front and back only along this edge.
2. Press the seam open.
3. Center the zipper, wrong side facing up over the seam.
4. Pin the zipper in place and carefully baste it to avoid fabric shifting as you stitch.
5. Use the zipper foot on your sewing machine. Remember to sew the zipper along the woven tape line on the wrong side of the zipper. Hand turn your sewing machine over the lower seam when crossing the zipper teeth.
6. Remove the basting stitches along the zipper seam.
7. Fold the pillow front and back, wrong side out, into its correct position with the zipper edge in its side position.
8. Place your straight sewing presser foot on your sewing machine. Pin the remaining outer pillow sides even, and sew these three sides by machine.
9. Clip your corners.
10. Open the zipper and reverse the pillow through this opening.

You may wish to have the freedom to insert a pillow form in and out of a pillow without the additional work of a zipper insertion. You do have another option for construction, an envelope closing for the back of your pillow.

Envelope Closure for Pillow Backs

Measure the pillow front. Cut two back sections that are the same height as the pillow. The shorter sides should be half the width measurement plus 3″. This additional width will allow for hems and an overlap.

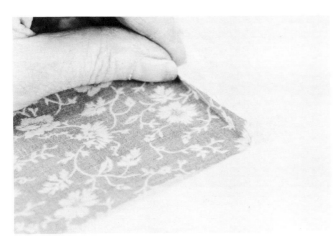

Press ¼″ over for a narrow hem on one long side of each back section.

Roll this under one more time.

Sew this with matching colored thread for a finished hem.

Position the two ends, overlapping along their finished edges, until they measure the same width as the pillow front.

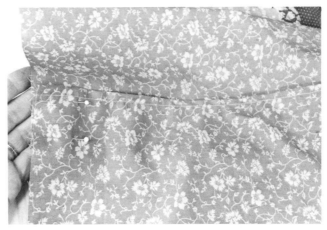

Pin these securely along the overlap edge.

Sew the overlap edge with a ¼″ seam.

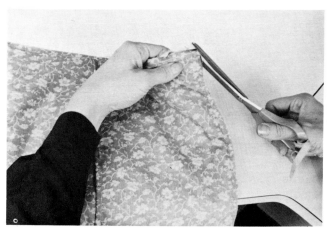

Before reversing the pillow, remember to clip your corners.

Pin the pillow front over the back, with right sides facing each other.

Reverse the pillow.

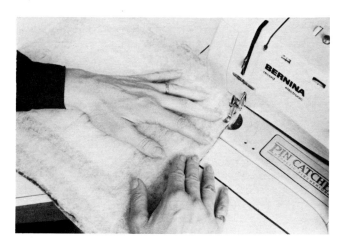

Sew the two front and back together. Stitch with a ¼″ seam allowance.

Insert your pillow form to finish the project.

Chapter II — Wallhangings

Wallhangings are the second most popular project for today's quilters. They make wonderful gifts, and are carry along projects for passing time in waiting rooms, or on the train. Working on a small project is ideal for relaxing in front of the television with the family at the end of the day. They allow the quilter to experiment with a wide variety of designs and provide a practical outlet for their efforts. Some quilt patterns are challenging, and provide an important step for skill development. However, your enthusiasm for a challenge may wane when required to make 35 for a bed quilt. The satisfaction you gain from completing smaller projects is an important reinforcement in your progression as an accomplished quilter.

There are multiple approaches to designing a wallhanging. Many wallhangings are small medallion quilts. You may choose to have a single block as your central motif, or a group of blocks that exemplify an interesting design created by the interplay of block units.

Your wallhanging can be square, rectangular, or with rounded corners. The shape can be modified to your specific decorating requirements. We will explore the many ways of bordering your wallhangings, and the options available to hang the completed unit.

Design Set on Point

One of the simplest, and most effective methods of transforming a block, or group of repeat blocks into an attractive wallhanging is to set the design "on point." This refers to turning the medallion section of the unit in a diamond like direction, and adding additional triangular sections to square the medallion off once again. Many block designs are drawn with this end in mind, like our pieced baskets and numerous tree patterns. Other traditional designs are simply more interesting when turned in this manner. Aside from the aesthetic qualities of this approach, the quilter can gain in a practical way from turning the blocks diagonally. The blocks will now be measured across its diagonal measurement to determine the width of your design. When a block is turned "on point," the diagonal measurement is approximately one and one half the length of the side of your block unit. This is a very effective method of making a little go a long way. When small blocks are turned "on point," they become large enough to create an ample sized medallion wallhanging.

The color photograph of my "Pineapple Sorbet" wallhanging is a good example of the simple method of turning a medallion "on point." Adding triangles and straight cut strips with a border, completed a very straightforward group of four blocks. The block unit is an 8″ pineapple design. In making the center of the blocks, I substituted a four-patch for the more com-

Pineapple Sorbet, original design by Author.

mon solid square. This provided a more effective color play across the four blocks. I think that setting the four block unit "on point," diverts the focal point from the block, thus placing the emphasis on the color interplay. The dominant color is yellow with a pleasing variety of pastels. Framing the four blocks with yellow's complimentary color blue makes all the colors of the medallion more vivid. Then I measured the side of the square unit created by the four blocks in order to determine the size of the triangles that I would need for the corners. The block side measurement will give you the size of the hypotenuse, or long side of the right triangle to be used in the setting triangles. If mathematics makes you nervous, think of this triangle as half a square, that has been folded diagonally in two. You have the long side and should be able to find the short sides by making a simple paper pattern.

Before cutting the triangles for your wallhanging, we must discuss that ever intimidating issue of "grain." Our fabric is woven with threads that run lengthwise of the looms, called the warp, and across the looms called the weft. The lengthwise threads are the strongest, and after the cloth is woven, these threads allow for no stretch whatever. The threads that run crossgrain, the weft, have a small amount of stretch. Fabric is weakest when stress is applied diagonally across the threads. This is commonly referred to as the bias of the fabric and has a great deal of stretch. In a practical application, you only need to remember that *the fabric edge that is parallel to the outside of your quilt, or wallhanging, should never be cut on the bias.* Ideally the fabric that runs even with the sides of your quilts should be cut lengthwise along or with the grain. The top and bottom of your quilt sections should be cut crossgrain. Stretching and puckering along the outer edge are caused by cutting these edges on the bias of the fabric. If you are using remnants that do not have a selvage to give you a clue to grain, pull gently along the outer edge, and you will quickly discover the stretching characteristics of your material. When measuring for the size of the corner triangles needed, use the unfinished outer block or medallion measurement to obtain the diagonal size of your triangles. This size will then include seam allowance.

I sewed my triangles in place to the outer corners of the unit. Wishing to reinforce the importance of my color selection, I again banded the edges with the same size strips of blue calico as used before. I added an outer edge of 6″ of yellow print to complete the medallion. I enjoy quilting and adding a good sized outer border gave importance to the size of the wallhanging and afforded me an adequate surface to add quilting stitches as a further design element. The thought process I employed in designing this simple piece shows that step by step you may make decisions based on your own needs.

Determining the width to use in a border can be a simple decision governed by how much fabric you have left. In my Christmas Pieced Star Tablecloth, I worked with odds and ends of Christmas fabric left over from previous projects. I was determined to keep this a scrap bag project. I chose to cut the lattice strips between the blocks from different calicos. By placing a four patch at the interesection at these lattice strips, I separated by otherwise mismatched bands. This maintained a pleasing scrappy appearance overall.

Christmas Pieced Star tablecloth, traditional by Author.

Select your fabrics of similar hue, and you should be able to change calico according to your needs, as the project grows and develops.

Mitering Borders

Adding a mitered border to a wallhanging or quilt enhances the design, as an artist frames his canvas. This is an easy technique, but will require about a half yard more of each of your bordering fabrics.

Measure the length of the sides of your quilt and the width of the border you plan to attach.

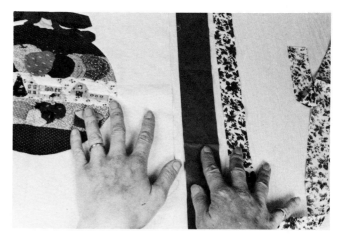

If you wish a border of multiple fabrics, and varied widths, such as a 2″ strip of color A followed by a 4″ border of color B, sew these lengths together first.

Seaming the multiple strips together will allow you to treat them in one operation when you miter. Your border length will include the length of the side of the wallhanging plus the width of your borders. Please remember to add those seam allowances. If your hanging measures 30″ square, and you are planning a 6″ wide border, you will cut four lengths for the border 6½″ x 42½″. Each side piece will include the length of the side of the quilt, plus the width of the two side borders with seams.

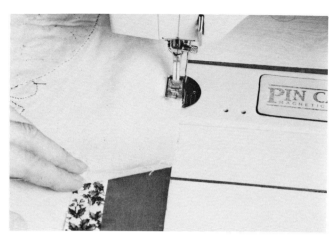

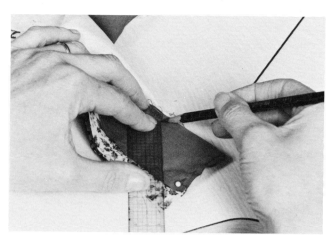

Position this border strip with 6¼″ extending beyond the side of the quilt. The two 6¼″ extentions should be falling freely in each of the four corners of the quilt. Sew the borders to the quilt side, stopping and starting within the seam allowance.

With a ruler, mark a line starting from the end of the seamline used to attach the border to the very outside point of the border.

You can trim the borders to the exact length after attaching them on the machine.

This line should be a diagonal as shown, starting at the seam attaching the border to the wallhanging, extending to the outside corner.

Grip the 6¼″ corner sections, with their right sides facing each other, and their short sides in line.

Pin along this line and sew. Be careful not to sew beyond the inside seam allowance of the quilt.

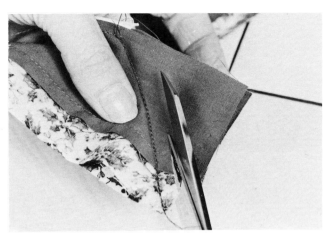

Peak to see if your stitching is correct on the right sides, then trim off the excess seam allowance from the border corners.

The mitered should be as shown.

Mitering is a most effective method to use when framing with a striped fabric. The outer edge of Lambee Pie, a wallhanging shown below, is a stripe,

Lambee Pie, original design by Author with Drunkard's Path pieced border.

and the miniature quilt shown on the small brass bed, has a small striped border as well. The miniature design uses the stripe to separate the center block from the Sawtooth border. Striped fabrics often feature a variety of designs printed side by side. They can offer many choices for border effects within the same cut of yardgoods.

Single and Multiple Straight Borders

If you do not wish to miter the border you can add a plain border of one fabric or multiple fabrics. Each border that is continuous from each outer edge of a wallhanging should be attached separately. For wallhangings, the simplest method is to sew the borders on the sides opposite each other first. Measure the sides. If one side is longer, and yet not a measurement that is over 42" wide, you should attach the borders to this side first. This should eliminate piecing the strips of fabric of your border material. Since most cotton fabric is woven on 44" looms today, be mindful of the order of attaching side borders to eliminate unsightly seams.

Sew the borders on the long sides first, from edge to edge with a ¼" seam allowance. Finally sew the border fabric to the two remaining sides. The last borders should include the width of the wallhanging, and the two border sections you have previously attached. For multiple fabric borders, repeat this procedure for each border.

A variation on a plain stripped border that I think is worth noting is what I like to refer to as the *Log Cabin Border*. More than likely, this was developed from the needs of a quilter, who discovered that she did not have a sufficient amount of any one fabric to make uniform lattice strips around all her blocks. With the use of odds and ends, you can surround each block in your wallhanging or quilt with a variety of narrow strips that conform to the standard order of construction of a log cabin design. By maintaining a light and dark arrangement, characteristic of log cabin blocks, or adding random fabric strips, you can effectively join an otherwise unrelated motif into a uniform grouping. The wallhanging pictured in our color section, Small World, was framed with strips attached working in a log cabin order. I sewed strips cut 1½" wide to opposite sides of the block. I then completed the picture by attaching strips to the remaining sides. Repeating this procedure once again, I completed the frame of the block, using small pieces of materials that I had used within the applique panel. When this technique is used in joining the blocks of a quilt, a strong secondary design is formed by the strip latticework. This is a simple procedure, but clearly demonstrates the creative possibilities when finishing a project. The enthusiasm you initially experienced when starting your work can quickly be rekindled when you stretch your repertoire of finishing skills.

Borders with Corner Blocks

Sewing a corner square to the edges of your quilt serves multiple purposes. This is an attractive accent that can repeat an important color or design motif into the border. Adding the corner accent square can stretch your border fabric and often eliminate the need for a large run of cloth for the outside edges. If you break the border up at the corners, or at regular intervals within the bordering edge, you will use less of your border material.

Seaming the borders that have an accent square in the corners is a straightforward procedure. Cut the bands whatever width you please, and the corner squares should be the squares of this measurement.

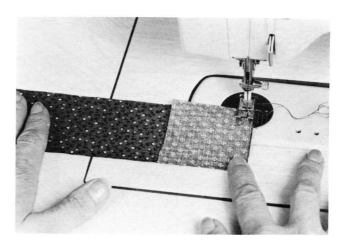

Sew one of the pieced or accent squares to one side of a border strip.

Cut the border sections for the wallhanging by cutting oversized lengths of strips, cut in the width you will be using.

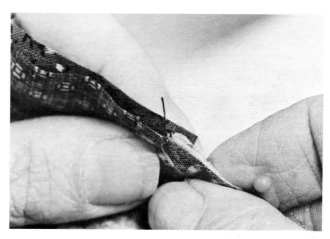

Attach the strip, carefully matching the corner to one of the remaining sides. If you layer the strip and corner seams folded in opposite directions to each other, as shown, they will be less likely to shift out of alignment as you seam.

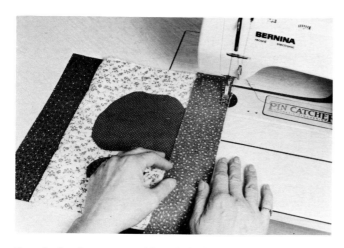

Sew the borders to two sides of the block unit, trimming the strips to their finished length after sewing them in place. Sew the bands on two opposite sides first.

Stop your machine sewing approximately 1″ before the line of attachment of the adjoining square.

43

Finger crease precisely the point on your band where the square should attach.

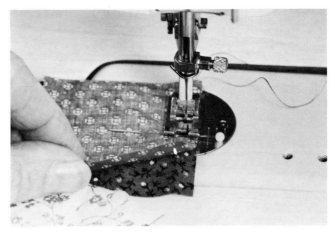

Sew the square along the crease line.

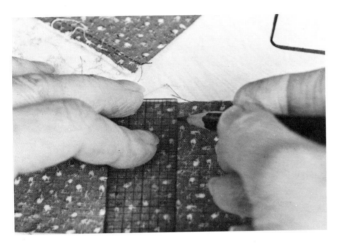

Add ¼″ seam allowance to this crease line.

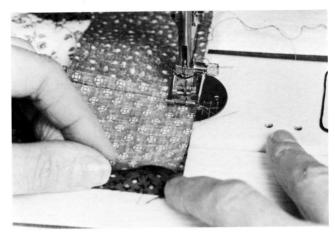

Complete the stitching of the band.

Cut off the excess material from the border strip.

Repeat this procedure for the final border.

This method eliminates the need for great accuracy in measuring and allows for the inevitable shifting of layers that your sewing machine will create when stitching.

Accent is the operative word here, and this method provides a pleasing affect. The Variable Stars set on the corners of my small Amish House Wallhanging adds in important detail to the overall appeal of this piece. Be careful, however; if your squares do not line

Amish House quilt, original design by Author with corner accent of variable star blocks.

up properly, there will be obvious flaws for all to see. If they do not please you at first, remember it will only take a small amount of time, a little patience and a seam ripper to correct the problem.

Pieced Borders

Borders are most commonly added for size, or as a design frame. A sadly neglected feature in many quilts, a border that is pieced or appliqued can transform a simple design to a blue ribbon winner. Pieced borders may seem frightening, but let's have a look at how to simplify their design and construction.

The first step is to accurately measure the sides of your wallhanging. The first factor to consider in planning your borders: does the side length divide by an even or an odd number? Since most of our pieced blocks are square, the length and the width of your quilt should be commonly divisible by either an odd or even number. For example, my Schoolhouse Wallhanging, shown in our color photographs, measured 33½″ x 33½″ without borders. I could, therefore, use any pieced unit in my border treatment that would measure 3″ when finished. I could not use a 2″ triangle, as I could not have a complete repeat

motif using this measurement. If your side lengths do not measure into nice even figures, what then? You will simply add a plain border of fabric that will yield the required measurement. Many medallion quilts and wallhangings have multiple plain borders just for this very purpose. The solid bands can restate a fabric or color used in the center unit of the quilt, and thus be an important design transition leading to the outside pieced edge. The Crimson Star Wallhanging, pictured in our color section, was not as cooperative as the Schoolhouse Wallhanging. When the four blocks were joined for the center, it measured 29″ x 29″ including seam allowance. I added a 2½″ wide red calico strips to all sides of the unit that gave me the 33½″ square edge that I needed to make my pieced border. One half inch of seam allowance was utilized when attaching the border. The Dogtooth border that I selected for this piece added a pleasing finish for an otherwise simple grouping of four repeat blocks.

When using a pieced border on an applique wallhanging, I do my planning in reverse. I decide what border pattern I would like for the edge, and how many units I will need for the repeat. I plan the inside of the wallhanging to fit perfectly within this pieced frame. I do not have to concern myself with a perfect fit here, as it is always easier to cut the background of the applique to suit the border. This is demonstrated by my Lambee Pie Wallhanging. I used a 3″ Drunkard's Path pieced border around the center lamb panel. The corners are solid squares, and the small wedge shapes of the Drunkard's Path design were cut from the background fabric used in the applique center panel. This made a scalloped setting for inserting my applique flowers and leaves.

An effective device for a border treatment is to repeat a design element in the border that appears within the body of the quilt. This will strongly unify the two quilt sections and carry the viewers eye back and forth across the design surface. Rainbow Daisy featured in our color photographs exemplifies this strategy. With sections left from the block units, I sewed triangular accents to the top and lower border seams. If I had selected fabrics of different values, I could have additionally achieved a spacial illusion of depth with this technique. This unites the border and the central panel into a strong analogous design

Dogtooth

Twist and Turn

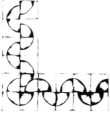

Drunkard's Path

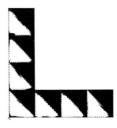

Sawtooth

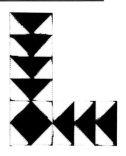

Flying Geese

without the need for sophisticated mathematical calculations.

Naturally, some patterns are easier to execute for border treatments than others. Changing the scale of a design may make a border easier to manipulate. The edge should look appropriate in size to the piece you are working on. In Sky Jinks, a small wallhanging shown below, I added a narrow rail fence edge. I had initially cut strips of 1½″ calicos for the rail fences; however, when these were placed around the edge, they overwhelmed the small design. Returning to the cutting table, I trimmed the strips to ¾″. I found that when the new strips were completed, their size was more appropriate for the design. Small sized units are much easier to work with in a border.

Sky Jinx by Author with rail fence border.

Planning Corners for Pieced Borders

You must be aware that when you turn the corner of a pieced or appliqued border design you may have a design shift or pattern merging. In most cases, when your units require an odd amount of sections for the border, your borders will turn without problems. In the case of my Schoolhouse Wallhanging, two sides required 11 triangular units, and the remaining sides required 13. In the event your unit divides evenly, your corners may need additional planning. The Dogtooth border required one section of its triangle to round the corner and maintain the pattern. Do not give up, when the corners require special handling, in most cases, you can work it out. You can anticipate the corner merging by a shaded diagram on graph paper. If the illustration does not clearly show the pattern to your satisfaction, cut out sample sized pieces without seam allowance from colored construction paper. Play with your border options and you should find a solution. My miniature quilt needed the motif of its Sawtooth

border to be reversed in the center of one side to allow for a smooth corner transition all around. This method is common for resolving troublesome corners.

When you have exhausted all your patience and the reference material available to you, there is still an option available for turning that pieced corner. Before you dismiss all faith in your logical abilities, be aware that some pieced designs will not turn the corners and maintain the same motif. Reach deeper into your bag of tricks and use a different corner design entirely. The Twist and Turn border detailed on the

My Patchwork House by Author with twist and turn pieced border featuring applique corners.

edge of My Patchwork House Wallhanging is a case of a motif that calls for corner planning. While the motif can be continued round the corner, inserting corner squares will always do the trick. Positioning an applique flower in all four corners made the design and the border work better.

Combine several blocks for a pieced border motif. Remove the background from a pieced fan, leaving the soft rounded edge of this pattern, and you can insert this design combined with others attractively into any corner.

In most cases, the pieced unit that you used within the wallhanging will be the best choice for the border unit as well. This motif will most assuredly be the perfect transition for design, linking the outside border to the central penal. Furthermore, without the addition of a plain band of bordering fabric to change your measurements, this geometric unit should be a perfect size to divide evenly into the side length of your project. Tumbling Bears, as pictured in our color section, was based on a simple 60 degree diamond. This diamond, when used in groups of three, forms the traditional Baby Block motif. Six sections of this diamond, when joined at a central point create a six pointed star.

Christmas Ball wallhanging, original design by Author using multiple mitered border.

Miniature quilt by Author.

Small World by Author, uses hard framed method for hanging and log cabin border.

Schoolhouse quilt by Author with sawtooth border.

Crimson Star wallhanging by Author using a dogtooth pieced border.

Rainbow Daisy, original design by Author with block unit repeated into the border.

Tumbling Bears, original design by Author.

Pieced Star by Author, traditional design bound with bias binding.

Three 60 degree diamonds, when outlined along their perimeter, form a hexagon. With these factors in mind, I used the size of three diamond units to make the hexagons for the applique backgrounds. Six diamonds formed the linking star for the center of the wallhanging. Bordering the piece was by far the simplest chore, since the basic size and unit of design had never been changed within the wallhanging.

Experimentation is the key to success when designing your borders. You are free to cut out actual shapes in various colored papers to represent your design options. Sometimes when you work with the full size paper samples, it is easier to see the impact of your design's scale. Problems will be more evident and by the same token, solutions will be found more easily. If the true size is awkward to work with in your limited workspace, scale the paper model pieces down to half size. Do not scold yourself for needing a physical model to work with instead of a pencil and graph paper. Architects and engineers have been using scale models for centuries to work through problem design areas. This approach is far superior to cutting up fabric and assuming that somehow everything will work when you sit and stitch. Remember Murphy's Law, a quilter lives within its limitations everyday. Anticipating a problem before it occurs is the beginning of the solution.

Appliqued Borders

Applied borders have a long tradition in quilting. A continuous vine that is never broken, represented life everlasting to our quilting forebears. Flowers and swags will provide a perfect compliment for the clean straight lines of a geometric medallion. The planning and mathematical requirements needed for executing a pieced border are still factors to bear in mind when working with an applique treatment. The units of your design must still fit evenly within the side and corner measurements of your piece. However, you should find these borders easier when planning your corner treatment.

The miniature quilt shown on our brass bed is a sample of the applique units that are most common in a sway or vine border design. The basic side section, used throughout the short and long sides is uniform in size. Measuring the side lengths, I determined that a unit of 3″ would work out evenly for all outside measurements of this quilt. In order to turn the sides smoothly, I found that a different size swag template with a sharper turn would be necessary to connect the starting and ending swags on adjoining sides. I drew this shape keeping a common pointed shape at the ends, but making the lower edge a tighter curve.

The first step in planning an applique border is to sew the background bordering fabric to all sides of your wallhanging or quilt. Measure the sides, and determine the size swag unit you will need to fit within your borders evenly. If you cannot draw a curved line or a straight line, use a flexible curve or French curve drafting tool. These are invaluable aids for drawing curved lines. I find it helpful to work with a piece of paper the same size as my border. This limits the drawing surface to the correct scale and keeps your sketches more representational of your finished project. Remember, you need only draw half of the swag shape if you fold your paper in two. Cut through the two paper layers when you are pleased with your shape, keeping an uncut folded centerline for the center of the swag. You will have a perfectly symmetrical shape this way. With a little experimentation you can create your own design for your wallhanging. Make a trial corner as well. Using shelflining paper or newspaper cut to the correct width and length, check your templates to see if they will indeed work correctly around the edge of your quilt. If you need to make an adjustment, make it in paper first.

When designing a flowered vine that will encircle your wallhanging, design the vine first. Find the repeat curve that will evenly subdivide the sides of your edge. Lay out a sample on paper. Your last concern will be to select a flower or leaf pattern that will connect with your vine. Don't make the vine disproportionately small for the leaf or flower templates. The vine should be in logical scale to the leaves. After all, the vine should support the vegetation that grows from it. Silly as this may sound, it is precisely this type of flaw that will make one design work and another look clumsy.

Quilted Borders

When you are planning the border finish for a quilt or wallhanging, never under-estimate the elegance of hand quilting. You can frame the design with a flowing cable, diamond grid, or select an elaborate applique design on the whole cloth, interpreted by quilting lines alone. The success of this approach is most effectively illustrated by the wonderful quilts of the Amish people. If you love the rhythm of your needle through the cloth and despair with math, this is the solution for you.

Select a quilting pattern that you like, and add a sufficient amount of fabric to the edges of your wallhanging to fit the pattern easily. You must now mark the design on your fabric.

Technology has presented the modern quiltmaker with many marking tools. We have available at most quilting supply stores today, washout markers and air dry marking pens. Both of these products can be used without problems if you follow the manufacturers directions. The air dry marking pens respond with the moisture in the air. Their marks may last on your cloth up to 48 hours. When the air is humid, the markings may last only one hour. Be aware of these limitations; this marker is suitable for quick jobs, or for experiments to test out a possible pattern. I use an air dry marker for outlining my signature on a project; I immediately follow this line with embroidery stitches for the final signature. The most common marker, the washout marking pen, will not fade from your fabric until you apply a generous amount of cold water, saturating the fabric. In some cases, you may not wish to wet your fabric, and thus find this product unsuitable. Quiltmakers have voiced concern as to the long term damage that the chemicals found in these marking pens may have on the lifespan of the quilt. It goes without saying, that if the quilt in question is earmarked for use in a college dormatory or in a baby's crib, it will have a limited lifespan despite the marker employed.

For marking most fabrics, I want a marker that will make a clear distinct line that can be easily removed. Pencil still answers my needs best. Visit an art supply store for an assortment of both soft and hard lead pencils. Soft lead pencils are denoted with a letter "B." A 2B is softer than a B, a B4 is softer than a 2B and so forth. With an adequate assortment, going up the range to a 5B, you can mark any design, while applying little pressure. This will permit you to erase the lines if you make a mistake. Keep the pencil tip sharp to allow for a fine line that will be covered with your stitches. For light colored fabrics or muslin, you will not require a soft lead. In this case, you should also have an assortment of H lead pencils. The grading system is similar for H (or Hard) pencils, with 3H being harder than 2H. For marking dark fabrics, buy silver pencils (with both hard and soft leads). You will find drafting pencils far superior to dressmakers pencils for marking cloth. You can maintain a sharp point, and your pencil sharpener will not devour these pencils as it would if you use dressmakers pencils. When you use a standard #2 pencil you cannot mark your lines without exerting an excessive amount of pressure on the pencil. This marks the fabric threads below the surface and makes removal of the lines a problem. When you use the B and H pencils as suggested, you will be able to easily remove the marking lines with a plastic or art gum eraser.

When planning the design for the border, remember that you can test out your pattern on shelf paper before marking your material. If your cable does not exactly fit within the border length, the least conspicuous place for making adjustments is the center of the border side. In all other forms of needlework, *compensation* is a standard and familiar term. In plain quilter's language, "fudging," or making it fit is a standard method of approach. The experienced quilter is not necessarily the stitcher who has mastered all those hard patterns with 106 pieces in each block. It is the quilter who has learned how to make it all fit together, compensating for pieces that may not immediately want to cooperate. If you find yourself one half cable short in a row, leaving a small space between all the cables on that side maybe the adjustment needed. An interruption of your pattern in the middle of a row, leaving a small space, is another good alternative. Inserting a heart motif between design sections can

sometimes allow you a perfect place for inserting your name, or the year of completion. If you find a solution to a problem, do not concern yourself with, "Is it ever done this way?" If it works, do it! You have now graduated to an experienced and innovative quilter. After all, Compensation is a technique taught in the advance needlework courses.

One of the simplest, and yet favorite filler patterns that is always an attractive border design is a diamond grid. You can make the grid line any distance apart, 2″ or 1″, whichever is pleasing to your own eye. This motif flattens the border and permits the design and quilting in your medallion to be more important. The diamond grid has the additional advantage of fitting within the size limitations of all borders.

Marking a diamond grid on your border fabric is an extremely easy procedure.

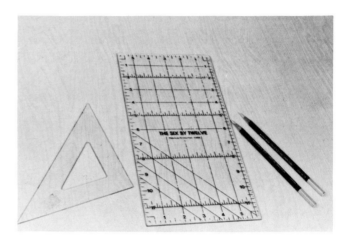

With the use of two inexpensive tools, a right angle triangle and a ruler, you can mark this pattern. A right angle triangle is available at most stationary or art supply stores; the size triangle is of no importance for most quilters needs. A clear, see-through ruler with grided lines from ⅛″ to 2″ in width will serve you well. Work on a flat surface, and use a marking pencil or pen that you can easily see.

Place the short sides of your right angle triangle even with the outside edge of your border. Slide the triangle so the right angle is cornering your border.

Mark your fabric along the long side or hypotenuse of the triangle.

Complete marking the border indicating the parallel grid lines that intersect your first set of lines. Maintain the same width between lines as you did in step 4.

Lay your ruler on this line, and mark parallel lines at the width you have selected. Mark the entire length of your border maintaining this angle.

You can continue this procedure around the entire outer surface of your wallhanging.

Lay your triangle with one of its short side on a line you have marked on your fabric. Mark along the opposite short side of the triangle edge as shown. This allows for the alternative lines forming the diamond shape.

The finished effect of this border is attractive and a wonderful place to show off your quilting stitches.

Trimming the Edges of Your Wallhanging

There are many accent trims for the edge of your wallhanging. They may include inserting lace, a ruffle, piping, or the delightful addition of prairie points. When adding one of these trims, anticipate their insertion, and do not quilt the outside inch of your work. The back, batting, and the front of the wallhanging can be trimmed to an equal length that is the finished size plus your seam allowance. When sewing lace or piping on the edge, refer to the first chapter for step by step directions.

The preparation and insertion of prairie points requires little time and skill. Prairie points can be used on inside seams of garments and wallhangings as well as the edge trim.

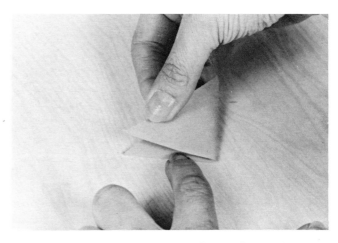

Press the triangles in half again diagonally as shown.

Cut an assortment of calico squares a uniform size. The sample shown uses 3″ squares. This size works well in most cases, however, the size can vary with your own needs.

An assortment of prairie points prepared in a variety of fabrics will be most effective.

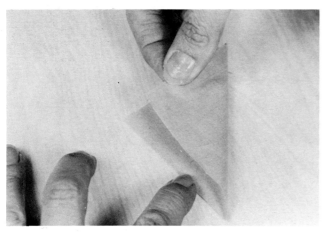

Press the squares in half diagonally, *with the right sides of your fabric facing out.*

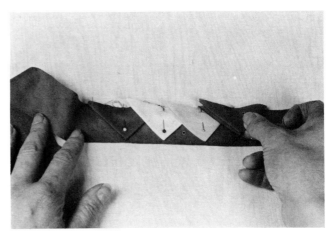

Position the raw edges of the prairie points along the raw edge of the seam. Lay the points overlapping each other at even intervals. Pin the raw edges of the prairie points securely to the edge of the insertion seam.

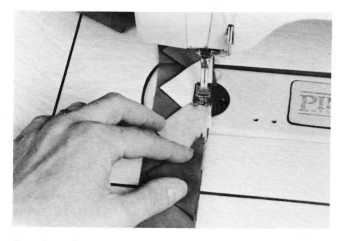

Sew the points to the seam. You may find it easier to set your sewing machine to a relatively long stitch length for ease in sewing through all the layers.

Attach the prairie points before joining an additional seam or binding to the same edge. This will eliminate movement and inaccuracies.

Flip the prairie points up by folding back the seam allowance. For the outside edge of a wallhanging, you will attach the points to the front of the hanging, folding the seam allowance towards the back of the wallhanging. Complete the edge by hand sewing the backing seam allowance over the front edge with a blindstitch. When including this trim for an inside seam, you can sew a strip or border to the seam that includes the points, treating this seam like any other in the unit.

Finishing the Edges of Your Wallhanging

There are a variety of methods that can be used successfully to finish the raw outside edges of a quilt or wallhanging. Each procedure has its advantages and limitations. It is up to the quiltmaker to select the method that works best and one which suits his or her needs. Wallhangings receive less wear than a bedsized quilt, and their smaller size is a determining factor in completing their edge. Essentially there are three options to finishing your edges: bring the backing forward, bring the front to the back, and bind the edge with bias binding. It does not take an experienced collector of antique quilts to know that quilts wear out first along their binding. Through the normal pulling and tugging on their edges. The stress of handling snaps the threads. This can be minimized by binding with fabric cut on the bias. Bias naturally will work best when finishing a curved edge. Ease in handling is one advantage to its application. Since its very nature is to stretch, it will therefore allow the threads to move when pressure is placed upon them. In the long run, with bias, the threads will experience less strain and will give the longest wear.

Refer to the first chapter on how to make continuous bias. When you want to attach bias to the edge of a quilt, the method that our photographs demonstrate is my favorite. It is recommended that the quilt or wallhanging be completely quilted before you attempt to bind the edges. This will eliminate the possibility of the layers shifting unevenly.

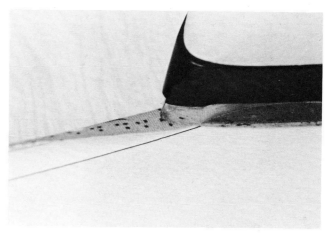

If you have cut your own bias and wish to even off the edges, you can mark a ¼″ line on a section of cardboard. Press one raw edge of your bias over the cardboard to this line. This will give you an accurate fold of ¼″ to seam in and compensate for any minor cutting inaccuracies.

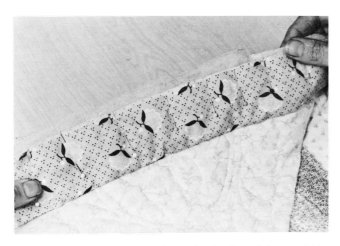

Cut away excess of fabric from the back and front of the quilt to allow ease in handling.

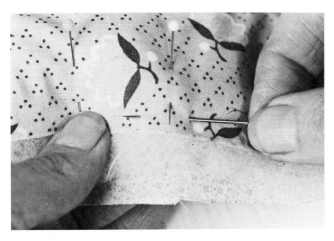

Baste this edge before trimming away the excess fabrics. Your basting should allow you to firmly draw up the three layers of top, batting and backing.

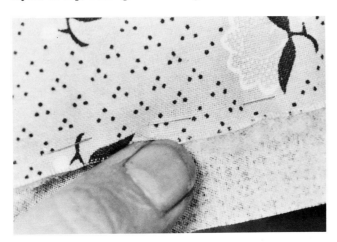

This will allow you to treat the edge as one layer and safeguard against small pleats forming when you sew the bias in place.

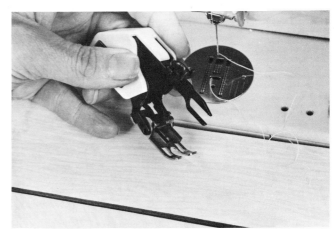

If you have a walking foot, or evenfeed foot for your sewing machine, this is the perfect time for its use. Cut your bias 1½" in width, or wider, according to your own preference.

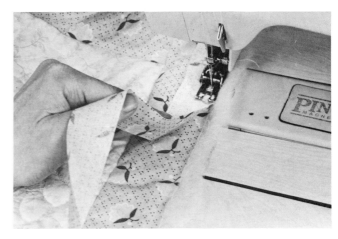

Machine sew the bias to the opposite sides of your wallhanging with right sides of your bias placed over the right side of the wallhanging. Line up the raw edges of all the layers. With your stitch length set on 10 to 12 stitches per inch, sew the bias in place with a ¼" seam allowance.

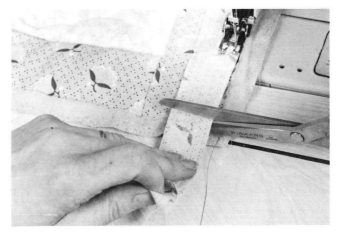

Sew the binding and trim off the excess to the length of your quilt side.

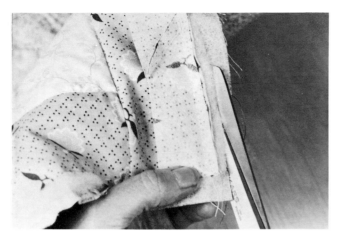

Remember to keep batting within the binding when you trim away the excess backing. This will help the binding to wear longer.

Complete the two remaining sides of the wallhanging by placing the bias on the two remaining sides. The ends of their binding should extend beyond the bias of the previously assembled side pairs.

Bring the binding over to the wrong side of your wallhanging.

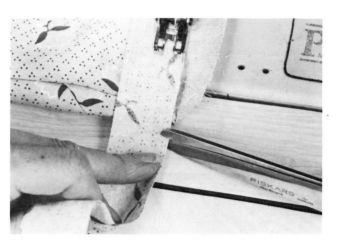

Sew these sides with ¼" seams.

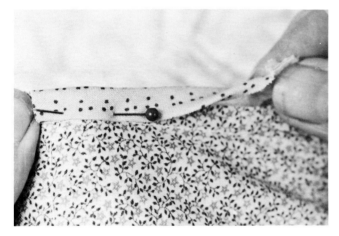

Fold under the ¼" seam allowance and pin this securely in place.

You will need to extend the bias at least ¼" beyond the sides.

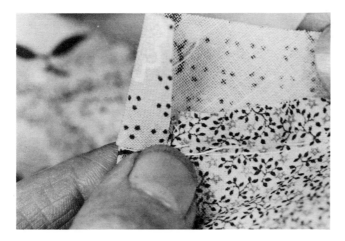

Tuck the short raw edges in as shown.

Pin this carefully before stitching.

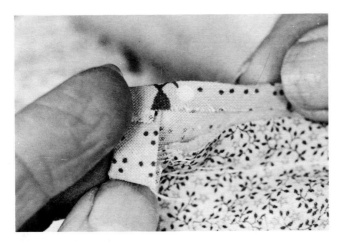

Bring the outer side raw edge over this fold.

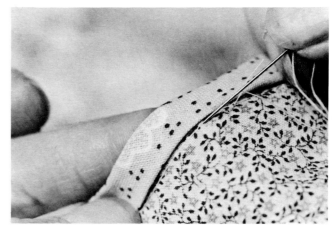

The photographs demonstrate the blindstitch or applique stitch utilized in this procedure. You should use a thread color that matches your binding. Insert your needle into the fold of the binding.

The outer corner should be in line with the width of the side.

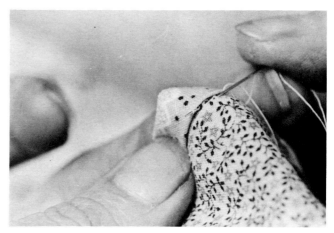

Return your needle into the quilt, directly in line with the binding stitch, slating your needle as you travel.

Bring the needle up into the fold of the binding approximately ⅛" from the first stitch. Continue in this manner using a single layer of thread.

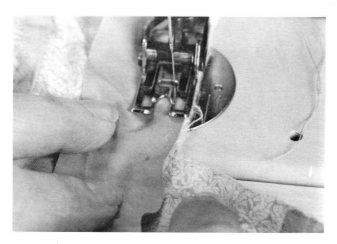

Sew the bias to the right side of the quilt. Your stitching should go to the point approximately ¼" directly in line from the convex merging point.

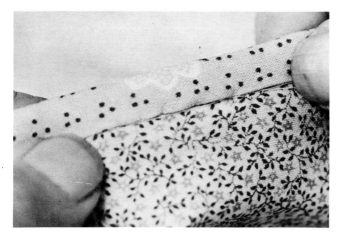

This stitch conceals most of your thread within the quilt. It will have little wear with use.

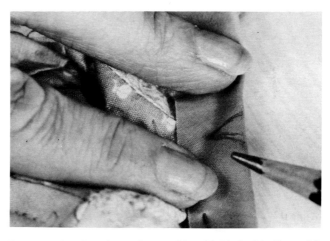

Remove the piece from the machine. Fold the binding with right sides facing each other together. Mark an angle on the bias within the seam allowance that is the negative image of the merging angles.

If you find straight corners awkward to bind, you may exercise artistic license and round the corners off. Place a circular shape, a teacup or wineglass, on the corner with two straight sides in line with the outside curved edge. Mark the curve as it continues around the corner. Remove your circular guide and trim away the excess fabric beyond your curve line. This is a particularly easy way to complete the edges of a rectangular placemat. This will allow you to sew the bias binding on in a continous motion.

When you are binding the edge of a curved border, as in the case of a scalloped edge, you must use a method that will take the excess binding out from the merging point of two convex curves. This is commonly found in the Double Wedding Ring pattern. The curved shape of this edge will require bias for its binding.

Sew with a small stitch length on your marked lines.

Starry, Starry Night, original design by Author curved edge bound with bias.

Cut fabric away within this angle as shown.

Replace the edge in the machine and continue sewing the binding on the edge working from the adjoining side of the point where the convex curve merges.

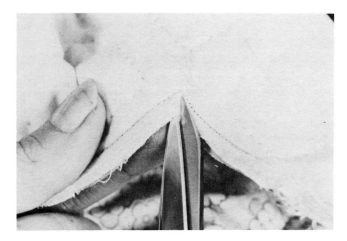

Cut the corresponding fabric in an angular configuration from the seam allowance of the quilt.

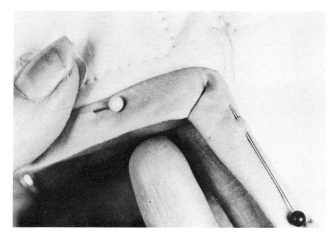

Fold the binding seam allowance over to the wrong side of the quilt to hand stitch. You will hand sew the two angular sides of the binding together on either side of the curve to connect the binding.

You will need to repeat this procedure for each scallop throughout the edge. This procedure takes some time and attention, but the end results are worth the effort. Complete hand sewing the angles closed when you finish the binding on the back side of the quilt.

Bring the Quilt Front to the Back to Finish

You may feel that you do not wish an additional trim on the edge of your quilt. Bringing the front over to the backing will certainly take little time and finish the job neatly. Problems may arise if you have failed to accurately mark and cut the borders. This is your last chance to correct mistakes. Measure the distance from the border seam to the outside edge of the quilt. Make this size consistant throughout the piece. Before completing your quilting remember, you will need at least 1″ of unquilted edge for ease in manipulating the outside edge.

Baste 1″ along the edge of the quilt. This will eliminate any shifting as you hand sew the edge.

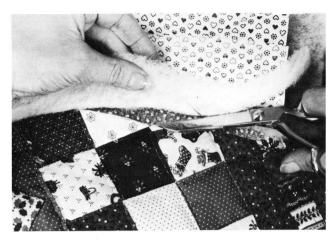

Bring the quilt front to the back of the quilt, and trim your batting ½″ from the edge.

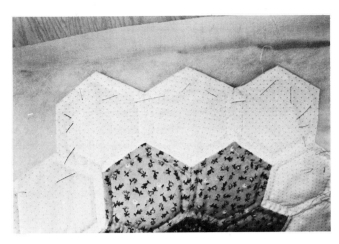

May I suggest the procedure of folding the seam allowance of both the quilt front and backing in against the wrong side. Turn the quilt front over ¼″.

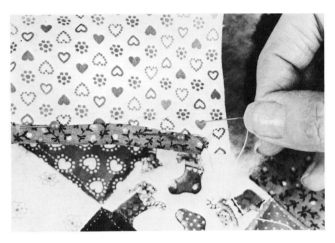

Roll the front ¼″ in to form a finished edge, and hand sew the edge in place with a blindstitch.

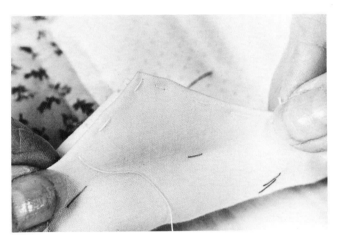

Fold the quilt backing over ⅜″.

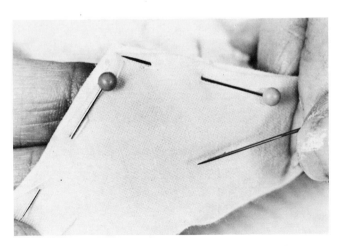

Trim the batting to the finished size of the quilt. Blindstitch the edges where they merge. Use thread to match the front of the quilt.

Finishing Irregular Edges of Quilts

A favorite pattern, Grandmother's Flower Garden, demonstrates a quilt edge that neither curves or ends with a straight line. This poses special problems in completing the outside edge. The particular configuration of this pattern along the outer edge is very pleasing to the eye. To bind this would be more than tedious; it could drive a quilter to knitting!

Bring the Backing over the Front to Bind

This is certainly an easy procedure for a wallhanging. However, when you are working with a bed-sized quilt, you may find it difficult to anticipate sufficient backing for executing this method. Since your quilt layers will undoubtedly shift as you quilt the piece, you may not have an adequate edge using the backing for binding. With small projects, however, this method is practical. Remember, as previously discussed, this does not yield a durable binding and should be limited to work that will not receive a great deal of handling.

When you wish to bring the back over the front, consider mitering this edge for an attractive finish.

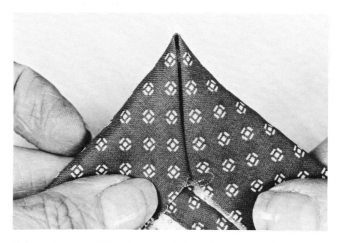

Bring the two sides of the backing adjacent to that corner over the front of the wallhanging. Pin in place.

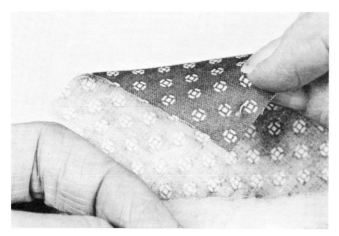

The secret to correct mitering is that your backing fabric must be precisely equal in size on all sides. You will find that an irregularity of ¼″ will prevent an even miter. The answer to this dilemma is simple, MEASURE AND MARK CAREFULLY. Fabric that is excessive should be trimmed away. In addition, while you need batting in the binding, you do not want it to be double in thickness at any point. Trim the batting to half of the binding without seam allowance. Fold the corner of your backing fabric under the corner of your wallhanging.

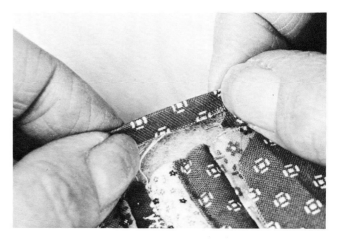

Turn under a scant ¼″ seam allowance along the edge of the backing.

The center of the fold should be even with the corner of the top unit.

Hand sew this seam allowance to the front with a blindstitch. Use matching colored sewing thread for blindstitching the front side of your wallhanging.

67

Methods for Hanging Your Work

The most common method to hang your wallhanging is with the use of a sleeve. A sleeve is usually a 3″ to 4″ band made from muslin or the backing fabric of the quilt. It is installed along the top edge of the quilt. This band is usually handsewed into place. When you are completing the edge of your quilt, stitch a sleeve made from the scraps of the quilt backing at the same time. This is certainly the most attractive method of sleeve construction. Place one long unfinished side of the sleeve band even with the outside top raw edge of the quilt. Place your bias binding over this edge when you attach your binding. Machine sew the top edge of the sleeve.

Bring the binding to the wrong side on the back of your quilt, and hand sew in place. Remember to use matching thread to avoid seeing your stitches.

Make narrow bands from your fabric for wallhanging loops. If you do not want to see the loops, set them down at least 2″ from the to edge. You can also stitch small plastic curtain rings to either side of your wallhanging. Since these rings may receive some handling, sew them in place with strong thread. I prefer dental floss to quilting thread when stitching these rings in place.

Finishing the Edges of Wallhangings Set in Hoops

Many hoop designs suggest a permanent installation. Surely there are times that this method is appropriate. You may, on the other hand, wish to utilize one hoop, replacing the design periodically. It is surely easier to store a hoop picture without the frame, and this also affords you the ability of cleaning the design whenever the need arises.

The method demonstrated by our photographs includes a ruffled trim that is sewn to the edge. The ruffle in this case was cut from continuous bias at a width of 3″. It was then ruffled with the use of the ruffler attachment on the sewing machine. The outside edge of the ruffle was then machine hemmed with a hemmer foot. The advantage of using bias will be evident when trimming a circular edge. Bias will allow the ruffle edge to stand out perpendicular to the outer edge of the design. It forms a delightful frame around the hoop. If you used fabric cut on the straight of the grain, your ruffle would fold over limply.

Prepare your design for hoop insertion at least one and one half inches larger on all sides than the diameter measurement of the hoop. When using a 14″ hoop, make a backing of at least 17″. It is not necessary to cut an oversized circle for the backing. A 17″ square will work nicely in this case. Complete all the design work, including the quilting. Open the wing nut of the hoop adequately and insert the design, taking care to keep the picture centered. Tighten the nut, after smoothing all the layers of the picture.

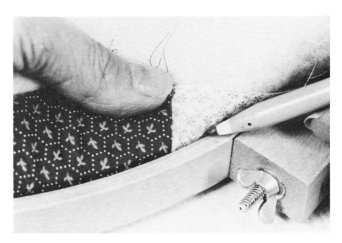

Using a marking pen, mark the wallhanging front along the back edge of the hoop rim.

Remove the picture from the hoop.

Halloween Hoop, original design by Author.

Position pins along the line you have just marked. Check to keep all your layers flat and smooth.

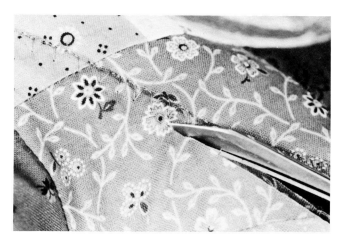

Trim away all layers that extend beyond the stitching line.

Set your machine to a wide zig zag stitch with a stitch length of 10 stitches to the inch. If your machine has an overlock stitch, a series of five straight stitches and one zig zag, use this stitch with an appropriate stitch length in preference to a plain zig zag.

Your design should now be the shape of your hoop plus the seam allowance of your stitching line.

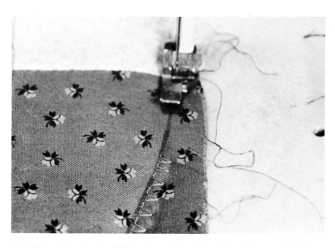

Position the marked line along the left side of your stitching line with the needle swinging towards the arm of the machine. Sew around the marked line.

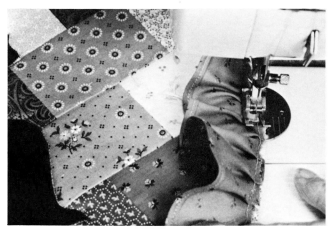

Sew the ruffle or trimming in place, using a straight stitch, to the outside edge of the hoop.

Join the two edges of the ruffles with a French seam as shown in Chapter One.

Measure the length of the sides of the Masonite™ and cut your Velcro™ to size.

Place the completed design into the hoop, and tighten the wing nut.

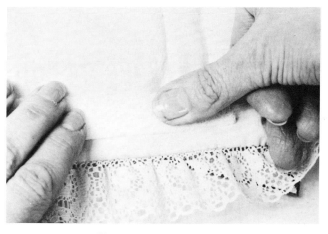

Peel the Velcro™ backing from one side and attach it to the board.

Hard Framed Wallhanging

There may be times that framing a block or design, and keeping the outside edges stretched is just the finish you desire. Surely you can always take your work to a framing shop and pay to have this treatment done by professionals. One problem with this approach, aside from cost, the picture cannot be removed for cleaning without totally disassembling the frame. I have a very simple method to achieve this look without the necessity of a woodcrafter or framer in residence. You can do it yourself. The cost is modest, and more importantly, the installation is not permanent.

You will require Velcro™ that has a self sticking finish. This product is readily available at craft and sewing stores. You will also need a piece of Masonite™ or thin ⅛″ plywood cut to the size of your wallhanging. You can get most lumberyards to cut any size you need of either of these materials.

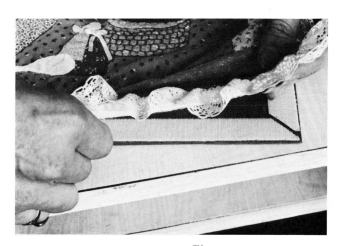

Peel off the companion Velcro™ section and attach it to the edge of your wallhanging. Firmly press the Velcro™ together, securing the wallhanging in place. You can lift the Velcro™, and make adjustments as needed. Attach a picture hanger or eyelet to the back of the Masonite™ for hanging or drill a hole.

Chapter Three — Patchwork Clothing

Blocks can be transformed into pillows and wallhangings as we have previously demonstrated, but have you considered taking your unfinished projects and using them to create a fashionable wardrobe? You can tailor your outfits from chic to country, setting a mood with fabric and designs. If your dressmaking skills are limited, you can be successful with only your patchwork know-how. With sewing experience you can become your own designer, incorporating patchwork into the construction of new garments. Sewers and non-sewers alike will appreciate tips for completing a tote bag without hand sewing. If your dressmaking skills only take you to selecting what looks best "off the rack," I have some suggestions that can give your wardrobe sparkle as well. One word of warning before beginning clothing projects, always wash your materials before you use them. This will eliminate shrinkage and expose the fabrics with unstable dye. When you use a lining fabric other than cotton, take care to wash this fabric as well. Iron all your materials after washing. You can hand or machine sew your projects, whatever your preference dictates. The important factor to guarantee a long life for a garment is quality in materials and workmanship. If you hand or machine stitch properly, you will have years of pleasure from your creations. It is for this reason alone that you should select classic styles that will be fashionable for many years to come.

Quilted Tote Bags

Tote bags are popular and functional items that can be for your own use or as gifts. I have organized my life by categorizing works-in-progress in tote bags that match all my outfits. Modern quilters have been accused of being a generation of bag ladies, but I for one would not trade the nickname for the convenience of this accessory. If you have a block or pair of blocks that are as yet unspoken for in your project plans, consider incorporating their use in constructing a quilter's tote bag.

In all of your quilted clothing items, you may be surprised to discover that it is usually easier to line a project than to use an alternate method for finishing seams. The ideal method for tote bag construction is to survive hard wear and frequent laundering. Machine sewing will be more appropriate for these conditions.

In order to provide a bag of adequate size, the first step should be to border the block designs with a band of fabric around all four sides. If the blocks are slightly different in size for the front and back of the bag, make the size adjustments in the bands to yield two panels that are of equal size.

Sew the front and back panels for the tote bag to a bottom section that is cut 3½″ wide and the length of the panels along the back and front sections. Sew this bottom section between the panels as shown.

Quilter's tote bag by Author.

Cut batting the same size as the outer tote bag shell. Cut the lining the same size as the outer shell. Machine or hand quilt the outer bag with the batting only behind the wrong side of the panel.

Cut two handle sections for the bag that are 6″ wide and 20″ in length.

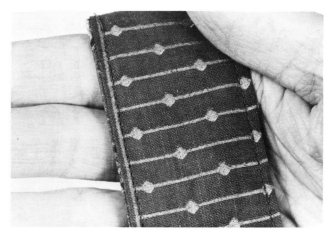

Machine sew ⅛″ along both long sides on the handles.

With right sides of your fabric out, fold the handle fabric in half and press.

Pockets should be cut double in length to create a self lining unit. Fold the fabric upon itself with the right side of the fabric facing each other.

Unfold the handle sections and bring the outside raw edge along the 20″ length into the center crease and press. Bring your outside creaselines together and press one more time. You should now have a 20″ length that is folded in four sections as shown, with the raw edges on the inside. Press.

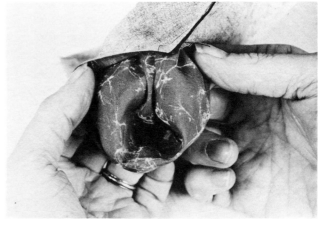

Machine stitch around the three raw edges leaving a length along one side open for reversing. Reverse and press.

Position the pocket on the lining and machine sew to the lining.

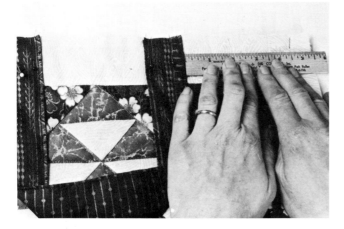

Measure the top edge of your bag from the outside short sides of the front bag panel. Position the handles an equal distance from each side. This measurement will vary with the size of your bag; however, the distance you select must be the same from both outside edges. The short raw edges of the handles should be in line with the unfinished top edge of the tote bag.

Sew the handles in place by machine with a ¼″ seam allowance.

Lay the handles flat against the front of your bag. Position the lining with right sides facing the right side of the tote, over the front panel. The handles should be between the layers. Pin the top edges together. Machine sew the two top edges of linings and bag together with ¼″ seam allowance. This seam will be sewn through many fabric thicknesses so set your machine for a long stitch of 8 stitches per inch. Your machine should have an appropriately sized needle of 90 or 14 to make the machine operate easily.

Lay the sewn bag sections on a flat surface, aligning the outer bag shell, and the lining sectioning facing each other. Take care to adjust the top seam open. Pin this seam together with the long sides of the tote matching.

You will sew one long side completely with ¼″ seam allowance. The remaining side you sew leaving an opening of approximately 5″ along the lining edge of the bag.

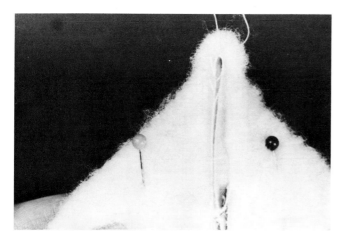

We will miter the lower edge of the bag to create a bottom section. On the front panel side of the tote, spread the side seam as shown in the photograph. Sew across the seamline that attached the tote bottom to the panels. Do not trim away the triangular section formed, as this will add firmness to the bag bottom. Repeat this procedure for the other side. You can stitch a similar triangular configuration in the lower section of the lining to create a lining bottom area. Reverse your bag. Machine sew the lining opening closed, turning the raw edges within the seam. Push the lining into the bag shell.

Press the top edge of the tote. Machine top stitch ¼″ along the outside edge of the bag. The topstitching will give a sharp edge to the bag top. The handles of this bag have been sewn three separate times during its construction. You will find these handles are strong enough to hold all your bag contents.

Whole Cloth Quilted Vests

The elegance of a whole cloth quilted vest is as lovely in clothing as it is when found in its bed-sized quilt cousin. With the selection of two cotton fabrics and accented with an attractive binding, you can enjoy the double pleasure of a reversible garment. Select your pattern one size larger than your "off the rack" size. This will allow sufficient ease for fit once you have completed your quilting. What a disappointment it would be to discover your vest does not fit after all your hard work! Select a low loft batting of cotton or polyester for this project. You do not want to add

weight to your silhouette with the look of a high loft batting. Prewash the materials for your vest, and select a lining of the same fiber content as your outer shell.

If you have selected two solid cotton fabrics, your next step before marking your materials is to sew the underarm side seams together for the lining and outer vest units. When dealing with clothing construction, you have a new seam allowance of ⅝″ to conform to. Additionally, in dressmaking with the larger seams it is advisable to open the seam allowance and press the fabric seams flat. Now that you have sewn the sections of the vest front and back together, cut your batting the same size as this unit. It will be easier to mark the vest before sandwiching the layers. If the lining material is chinz or has an interesting design motif, you may simply wish to quilt along the design outline. This would eliminate your need for marking. When you wish to work in a classic design, like a feathered wreath with a background filling grid, take out the marking tools for the job. For additional ease, you can tape the vest front to a surface with masking tape. Your shoulder seams should be unsewn, and the vest should therefore lay flat. Select the central design motif placement and mark this on your vest back. A smaller motif repeated from this design may be marked on both or one vest front. Fill in the background with a diamond grid, or clamshell filler pattern as discussed in the previous chapter (Wallhangings). When your marking is complete, layer the batting and lining behind your vest front and pin in place. Since you have several outside edges on this garment that are cut on the bias of the material: the armholes, neckline, and shoulder seams, it is advisable to baste the project working in a diagonal manner and at close intervals. There is an old adage that states that "You can never be too rich or too thin." I would like to add to this phrase, "And never baste too much!" Basting is the key to success when quilting. Since the shape of this project does not easily quilt within the confines of a hoop, it is all the more important to baste thoroughly.

Quilt this project as you would any other, stitching from the center, in this case, the center back of the vest working out to the vest front. You can quilt out to all the edges except the shoulder seams. At the shoulder seam, maintain a ⅝″ seam allowance that is free from stitching to make seaming easier.

Trim the batting away from the shoulder seam area before attempting to join the seams. Sew the front shell fabric together along the shoulder seam with a ⅝″ seam. Turn the lining side raw edges in, and hand sew these edges together using a blindstitch or applique stitch. You can add quilting stitches through the shoulder area for additional strength after completing the shoulder seam. Complete the project by making your own bias binding of 1½″ in width using the Continuous Bias method given in Chapter One. Sew this by machine or by hand to the right side of the vest. Fold the raw edges of the bias under, and complete the

Wholecloth quilted vest by Author.

project by blindstitching the bias to the wrong side of the vest. If you use matching thread, and a small blindstitch, your vest will be reversible. Rounding off the corners of the lower front of the vest will make it easier to attach the bias in a smooth continous manner. If you have a free arm sewing machine, you can utilize this feature when applying the binding to the armholes.

Decorative Seam Binding for Clothing

This attractive finish will make your garment reversible, and it adds an accent line to your silhouette. Binding the seams is a variation of a french seam finish. When you plan on implimenting this technique, consider the order in completing your seams. First you should complete binding the inside seams of your garment that are perpendicular to the outside edges. For example, you would complete binding the shoulder and side seams of a vest before you bind the outside and armhole edges. In this way, your binding will finish the raw edges of the garment as well as the short raw edges of your binding. The binding that you will use for this procedure should be made from the continuous bias method detailed in Chapter One. If you make a tube from an 18″ square of fabric, you should have sufficient 1½″ binding for vest sizes up to and including a ladies size 14. Furthermore, this binding can be a striking accent when used to finish a whole cloth vest. You should use this method after you have completed the quilting on all the separate sections of your garment. The sample shown in our color photographs is the Amish vest. The vest surface is embellished with "Flying Geese" sections of varied solid color cottons. The binding is an important accent and outlines the vest dramatically.

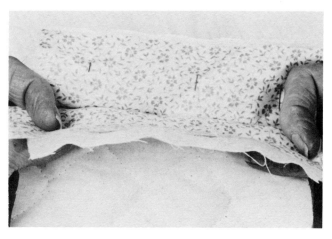

Position your seams with wrong sides facing each other and with the raw edges in line.

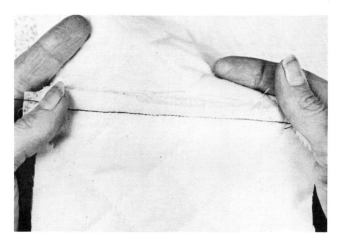

Sew the seams with a ½″ seam allowance. Trim the seams to ¼″.

Amish Flying Geese vest by Author.

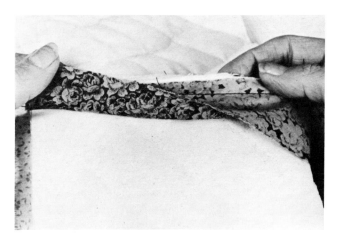

Sew bias to the front side of your seam with a ¼″ seam allowance.

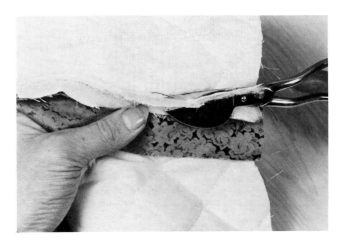

Fold the binding over the garment seam.

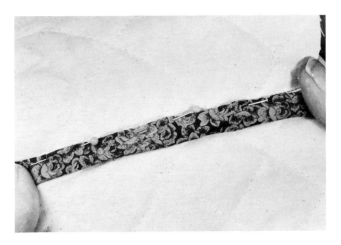

Turn ¼″ seam allowance of the binding over, and complete the procedure by handstitching the binding with matching colored thread. Sew with small applique stitches to provide adequate strength to the garment.

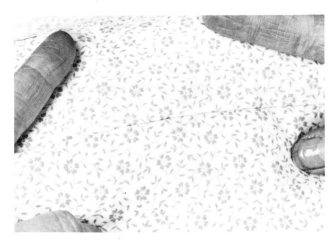

On the lining side of the vest the seam finish is not visible.

Lining a Patchwork Vest

In clothing construction, it is advisable to eliminate the necessity for bindings and unnecessary facings by finishing a garment with a complete lining. Aside from the speed and the elimination of hours of handstitching, a lining provides the garment with a tidy inside appearance, covering the construction lines of the outer shell. This is a great advantage with patchwork clothing. With the awareness of multiple techniques, modern quilters frequently incorporate strip quilting, seminole patchwork and applique all within one design. Furthermore, the garment is sturdier when the construction seams are conciled, minimizing their wear. When your vest is constructed of many seams, consider eliminating the batting. You can cut your garment foundation of muslin, or use a paper foundation that can be torn away after the outside shell is completed. Multiple seams can make your garment heavy for normal wear without the inclusion of even a low loft batting. Our color photos show my "Flying Geese" vest accompanied by a coordinating skirt. This is an interpretation of the same design used in the Amish vest; however, it did not include batting. The vest and skirt are light in weight and serve my needs nicely for summer wear.

Before selecting the fabric you will use for lining, let us consider the function a lining provides for a garment. Linings for most "off the rack" clothing are made of slippery material. This provides the wearer less difficulty in sliding the garment on and off. If you are wearing a knitted sweater or woolen shirt, a jacket lined with cotton can be difficult to put on. Frequently, quilters select a favorite calico cotton for lining that is strong, but will not permit the ease in putting the garment on and off that a classic lining material will provide. If you allow that you may some day wear a

Flying Geese skirt and vest by Author.

sweater under your quilted vest or jacket, I would strongly suggest a traditional lining fabric for this purpose. The two piece "Flying Geese" outfit I previously referred to was intended for wear on hot days. I never planned to wear the vest over a sweater, and furthermore, wished a comfortable outfit for warm weather use. In this case, a cotton lining was my best choice. Lining fabrics that are slippery are usually made of synthetic fibers or silk. These fibers inhibit the radiation of body heat and are quite uncomfortable on hot days. Don't be put off by the many factors you should consider when undertaking a clothing project. The variety of fabrics and design will permit you to make a garment that will be best suited to your own specific needs.

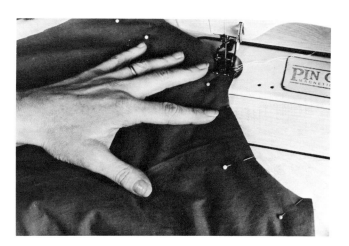

Position the lining over the garment shell with right sides of your fabrics facing each other. Pin the layers together, matching the outer raw edges all around. Sew the center-front edges and lower bottom edge together with a ⅝" seam allowance. Sew the neckline on the vest front and vest back as well with ⅝" seam allowance.

Sew the completed outer shell of your vest together with a ⅝" seam allowance, stitching the underarm seams only. Open and press your seams flat.

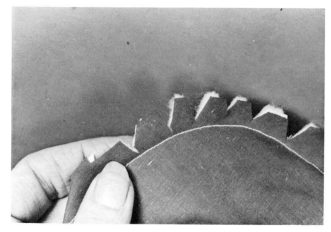

At rounded edges clip into the curves with a V shaped cut. Remove excess fabric within this cut to allow for a smooth smaller curved area after reversing.

Sew the lining, cut in the exact manner as the outer shell together, stitching the underarm seams only. Open and press these seams flat.

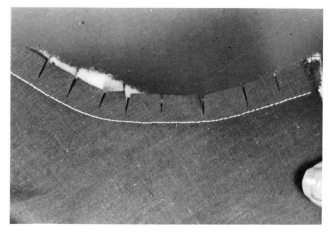

Clip into concave curves up to the stitching line to allow these areas to reverse smoothly.

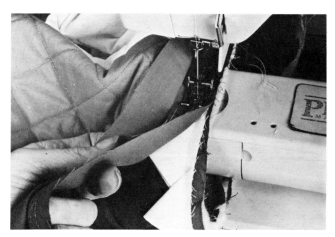

The sample vest that our photograph illustrates has a decorative armhole trim of "Prairie points," with binding. If you were not trimming the armhole edges, you would seam the armholes as well with a ⅝" seam allowance. *The only opening you would use in this case would be the four shoulder seams of your vest.* Since our sample includes an armhole trim, we can reverse the vest, after trimming across the seam corners of the vest front. Take care to cut into the curves of the vest, down to the seamlines before reversing. If your outer vest is thick trim off excess material more than ⅜" within your seam allowance. If your vest includes batting, trim this way ⅛" beyond your seamline. The variation in trimming your seams is termed "grading." This will allow for less fabric bulk on the garment edge and thus provide for a sharp outer edge. With the inclusion of an armhole trim, the shoulder seams of both the garment shell and lining can be sewn by machine in one operation. Carefully align the layers with the neckline seam pressed open and sew the vest shoulder front and back together with a ⅝" seam allowance. Press the seams flat, and trim away any batting that may be within this seam.

Position binding over the trimming and sew over the raw edges with ⅝" seam allowance.

Trim away the excess fabric from the seam allowance and binding, grading the layers to eliminate bulk. Complete the edge by turning the raw edge of your binding and blindstitching this in place by hand. Machine topstitch the outside edge of your vest after pressing to give the vest a crisp edge finish.

If you are using a standard commercial pattern for your garments, you must assume that all the outside seams were designed for a ⅝" seam allowance. If you are using a pattern designed for quilters this seam allowance may have been reduced to an outside edge of ¼". You should read the pattern to determine this. The shoulder and side seams in all cases should be ⅝".

When you have not incorporated a trimming on the armhole of your vest, you will be following the method suggested for leaving the shoulder seams on both vest fronts and back open. Cut the excess seam allowance away as previously suggested, and clip into the curves up to the seamlines before reversing. Inexperienced sewers are usually timid about clipping up to the seamline for concave curves. Reassure yourself that you will not be able to reverse the curve without preforming this procedure. The deeper and sharper the curve the more frequently you must cut

Position the armhole raw edges in line, as well as the shoulder seams. Pin the armhole edges together and machine baste this edge within ¼" from the outside edge. Insert the trimming that will be used in the armhole area, sewing this in place by machine.

Christmas vest, original design by Author with prairie points along armhole for accent.

into it to reverse its shape. After the garment is reversed and pressed you can reinforce the outer edge by topstitching ¼" to ⅛" with your sewing machine. This will give the outside edge a sharper definition, and prohibit the lining from rolling into view when the garment is worn. It is important to stop your seams on the necklines ⅝" away from the outside edges. This will provide necessary space to comfortably slide your hand into the opening for reversing the garment. Place your hand into *one* of the back shoulder openings and gently slip the layers through this space. *The entire vest will reverse through this one opening.*

Align the outer fabric of the shoulder with front and back facing each other, and machine sew these together with ⅝" seam allowance. At the shoulder line, stop and start your seams ⅝" from the outside shoulder edges. Turn your vest to the wrong or lining side. Press the shoulder seams open and flat for the least bulk within the garment. Turn back the lining seam allowance so the seamlines are abutting. Hand sew the lining seams together with matching thread to complete your lining.

Press the outside edge of your vest for a sharp finish line. If your vest has batting within the edge you may find it beneficial to topstitch the edge by hand to prevent the edge from rolling. This can be done inconspicuously with a single strand of quilting thread.

Quilted Jackets

The approach to finishing jackets is essentially the same as that used for vests. You can complete the seams by binding the edges with a decorative trim or construct the garment to allow for a lining shell to be inserted after your patchwork has been completed. When lining a jacket, you should consider the importance of selecting a slippery lining fabric. Construct the lining shell in precisely the same manner as the outside jacket unit including the insertion of your sleeves. You can machine sew the outside edges of the jacket and lining together along the front and lower sides. Place the lining with right sides over the front of your jacket and sew the layers together with ⅝" seam allowance. Reverse the lining through the jacket neckline. Bring the lining over to the right side, and complete your jacket by finishing the neckline with binding or with a collar attachment. The lower sleeve edges can be finished with binding or by turning their raw edges in against each other and hand sewing these edges. This will provide a jacket that can be reversible if you desire, and a jacket with little hand sewing. Throughout the discussion of finishing patchwork clothing, I emphasize a minimal amount of handstitching to finish the garment. This is recommended for a practical lifespan of the garment. Machine made clothing is usually stronger. Furthermore, if the garment does not represent the labors of weeks or months, you are more likely to wear it frequently. For a quilter, our wearable projects offer a happy new addition to our craft.

Patchwork Skirts and Dresses

The first garments that most quilters attempt are vests and jackets. As an experienced dressmaker, I would always suggest that a new sewer begin clothing construction with a skirt. Skirts are easiest to fit and take the least sewing know-how. Applique and patchwork are the ideal compliment for lightweight skirts, and with confidence gained through experimentation you can quickly extend your patchwork garments to include heavy weight fabrics of wool, corduroy, and velvets.

Pattern selection is the key to success for any patchwork garment. The patchwork that you wish to include in your design will in most cases be square or rectangular in shape. You can assemble a band of squares to insert into a skirt's lower edge or to be positioned vertically in a skirt front. A vertical accent line will, in most cases, be more flattering to the silhouette and require fewer patchwork units. Try a horizontal band of seminole strips or a row of "Flying Geese." In most cases, you will find it best to select a pattern that is constructed of rectangular shaped sections rather that A-lined shapes. The back of the pattern envelope will have a representative drawing of the pattern pieces that form the design. Study these shapes for your patchwork strategy. You want some fullness to the skirt, but not yards and yards of fabric that will overwhelm or hide your design. Once you have selected your pattern, some modification should be considered. Skirt patterns all list the finished lower width of the skirt. You can modify this measurement so that a complete repeat of your pieced design will fit evenly into this measurement. For example, the front lower edge of one skirt may measure 26". If you adjust this measurement to 27½" you will be able to insert a com-

Quilted jacket, and "off the rack" dress trimmed with pieced Carolina Lily design by Author.

plete repeat of 3″ sawtooth units. The additional fullness is so little that the integrity of the original skirt design will not be altered.

When you wish to accent your garment with a pieced section, insert the panel with inside seam. Try to eliminate appliquing your patchwork on to the garment as machine sewn seams will be stronger and give longer wear.

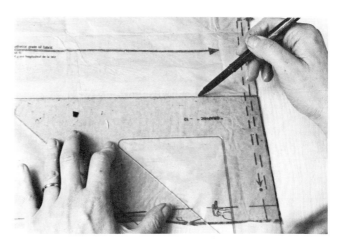

Mark its location on your pattern piece.

The panel that I wished to insert in the skirt was completed to conform to the unfinished skirt length.

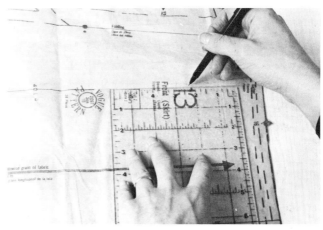

Using tracing paper, make two new patterns using the original as a guide that represent the two adjacent sections on either side of the patchwork.

The skirt used in this demonstration I designed for a patchwork insertion positioned off center in one front panel.

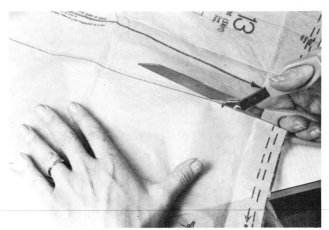

Cut the two patterns out and remember to add ¼″ seam allowance to the seams of the two patterns to allow for the seam in your patchwork.

Once you decide where the patchwork will be located, you should measure the patchwork panel.

Cut the side sections of your fabric using your new patterns. Lay the sections on a flat surface for assembly.

Sew through these three layers, attaching the panel and the lining in one operation.

Cut a lining section of a lightweight fabric the same size as your patchwork panel. Maintain a grainline on this panel that is in accordance with the garment. If the skirt front is cut lengthwise of the grain on your material, the lining section should be cut in this direction as well.

Lay the panel flat with the seams pressed within the lining section.

Position the patchwork panel with right sides facing the skirt section and pin in place. Position your lining with its right side facing the wrong side of your skirt as shown.

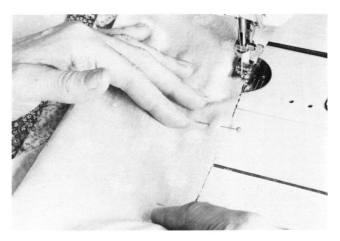

Pin the opposite panel side to the adjacent skirt section and sew.

Lay the lining with its ¼″ seam allowance over the panel on the wrong side of the skirt. Pin the lining flat against the panel with all seams edges pressed within the lining.

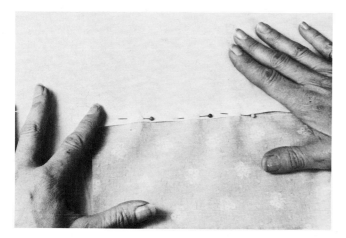

Finish the panel by hand sewing the lining to the wrong side of the skirt as shown.

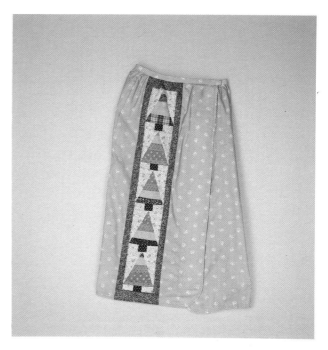

Inserted patchwork panel of Pinetrees by Author.

Unicorn applique on "off the rack" skirt.

Lining the patchwork inserts of your garments will protect the delicate ¼″ seam allowances from the wear and tear of frequent laundering. Garment sections that are directly attached to the patchwork should be given ¼″ seam allowance at their points of attachment.

When you wish to incorporate patchwork into dresses, follow the same design requirements that we followed to select a skirt pattern. If the dress pattern was designed for patchwork accents containing a yoke, wristband or skirt band, simply follow the pattern directions. In the event the pattern does not suggest this treatment, look at the pattern envelope and determine if the design lends itself to this approach. If the skirt or dress sections are squared off with a minimal amount of fullness, your patchwork can be a wonderful addition.

Applique can be added around the neckline of many garments, as well as on sleeve and skirt sections. Machine or hand applique when correctly executed can give many years of wear on a garment. When I use applique in a quilt or wallhanging, I trim the background fabric away beneath the appliques, main-taining ¼″ seam allowance. This is recommended for several reasons. It prevents the background fabric from greying the colors of your appliques. It allows the batting to come up under your appliques, and thus have the same layer characteristics are the other quilt sections. You will additionally have the freedom to quilt over the appliques as they will have the same thickness as the other quilt areas.

I believe that this approach is inappropriate when adding appliques to clothing surfaces. The garment itself will be the applique background. Cutting this away from beneath the appliques would surely weaken the garment. The solid foundation the garment provides will serve the same function as a lining to protect the applique seam allowances during laundering. To prevent the background from greying your appliques you can line these shapes with an interfacing or a second layer cut without seam allowance of muslin.

Select the materials for your applique as you would for a quilt project. You will find greater ease in handling 100% cotton fabric that has been prewashed for most applique projects. With a garment you have the advantage of working with a completed foundation before adding the surface design. Pin the appliques where you think they will look best, step back and see if you find your ideas pleasing. If you hold the appliques with a touch from your gluestick you could try the garment on and preview the finished effect. The unicorn fantasy design provided a wonderful summer treatment to the white wrap skirt featured in our color photograph. The multicolored design permits me to wear this skirt with every colored blouse in my wardrobe. Remember for those fall and winter weight fabrics, 100% cotton can include corduroy and velveteen for your applique selection. It would naturally be easier to use machine applique when applying a heavier weight fabric. Silk and lame are also wonderful fabric choices for patchwork, and applique. Read the manufacturers suggested washing directions for these fabrics, and don't be afraid to experiment. A wide spectrum of color and texture can only add to the richness of your garments.

Patchwork for "Off-The-Rack Clothes"

Although my first love was dressmaking before I was introduced to quilting, there are times when I do not have the time to make a garment from scratch. If I find a dress that is well made and that fits my pocketbook and figure, I will buy it and then consider it for quilted embellishments. Necessity off times being the mother of invention, I have additionally used my quilting know-how to cover a stubborn stain or update a garment that had past its period of stylishness. Whatever your reason, open your closet and look at the potential candidates for "Patchwork Pygmallions." Applique is the obvious choice of technique to employ for this purpose. Stretch your skills to include pieced designs as well as traditional appliques. The blue sundress shown in our color photo, was a wonderful candidate for bright yellow Carolina Lily flowers. Repeating the flower to the neckline creates a continuity of color and design throughout the garment. With a little time, and a great deal of pleasure you can add your own individual signature to mass production garments.

Pockets are wonderful areas that you can highlight with your quilting palette. The white sundress in our color photo was brighted by calico pockets made from the ever popular Grandmother's Fan pattern.

"Off the Rack" clothes featuring Fan pockets and Carolina Lily Pieced flowers.

Sew the fan sections together.

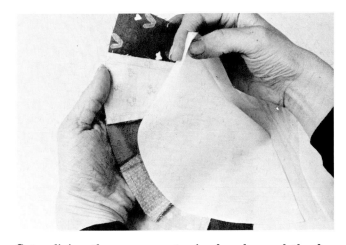

Cut a lining the same quartercircular shape of the fan section.

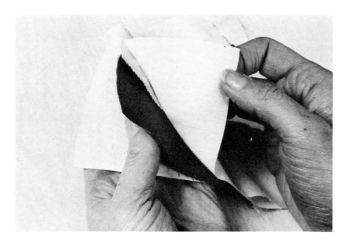

Position the lining over the right side of the fan section.

Sew around the arch of the fan shape using a ¼″ seam allowance. Sew down one straight side of the fan as well. Reverse and press this section.

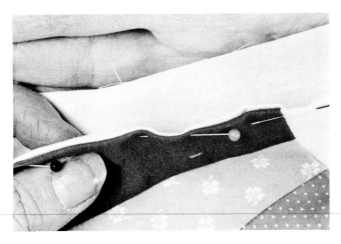

Pin the remaining straight side and close with hand or machine sewing.

Position the pocket on the garment.

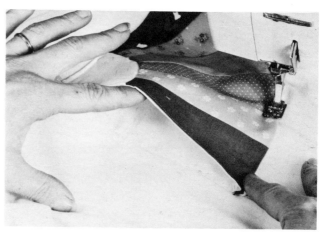

Sew the pocket in place on the garment.

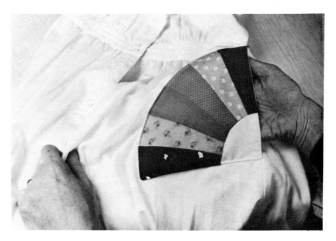

Leave the straight side parallel to the dress side seam open.

If your sewing machine has the option of dropping the feed dog, do this procedure when anchoring the pocket at the beginning and at the end of its attachment. Your machine model may have a darn setting for this purpose; refer to your owners manual for this instruction. Dropping the feed will allow you to make multiple stitches in one spot, without the machine moving. This will secure the pocket edge, and eliminate unsightly machine backstitching. Start by sewing five stitches or more, raise the feed up and procede to sew the pocket, repeat this procedure at the end to secure the opposite edge with the same reinforcing stitches.

Many traditional blocks can be adapted for pocket designs. Add a corner fold or make a slight modification to the block shape to allow easy access for your hand.

Patchwork Accessories

A patchwork collar or belt can go far to transform a plain "Off the Rack" garment into a whimsical fashion statement. Miniature blocks can readily be incorporated into a collar or belt, as well as using the vast assortment of strip pieced and applique techniques. The wonderful advantages to these projects is that you do not have a size problem, and the projects take relatively little time to complete. Most commercial pattern manufacturers offer patterns in their craft section for collars and belts. The patterns are adapted for all adult sizes and come with an assortment of styles. While one design may immediately inspire a stitching strategy, with a little experimentation you will be happy indeed that you have many types of collar configurations to work with.

Collars for all occasions, pieced, appliqued, and strip quilted by Author.

For strip piecing you can cut the outside shape from a newspaper pattern. This will eliminate the necessity of a batting or fabric foundation. The paper will give you a sufficient base to apply your strips to, and will easily tear out from the seams when you have completed your outside shell assembly. When inserting patchwork, follow the procedure suggested in our photo demonstration of inserting a panel into a skirt. For applique you can machine or hand sew the design to your color foundation fabric. In most cases, it will

be simpler to finish your collar by lining the entire shape. Select a cotton fabric lining in this case, as a slippery fabric will not stay centered during wear. Sew the outside collar section together attaching the shoulder seams. Open and press the shoulder seams flat. Sew the lining together in the same manner, keeping in mind that most garment construction seams are $5/8''$. Position the lining over the outer shell with the right sides of your fabric facing towards each other. Stitch around the neckline curve and around the outside edges, leaving an opening along one straight side, preferably along the collar back. Clip the curves and cut across the angles as demonstrated in Chapter One for reversing a pillow corner. Press the collar and topstitch to insure a sharp outer edge. The collars grouped in our color photograph show the variety of styles possible for quilters. With one sweater or blouse, you can create and entire collar wardrobe for every occasion.

Belts are also exciting opportunities for patchwork designs. Belt patterns are also available for purchase from commercial pattern manufacturers. However, since this is one item that we all have samples readily available to use, you can always trace a shape using a favorite belt in your wardrobe. In most cases, it will be more appropriate to work with a belt style that closes with buttons, hooks and eyes, lacing, or by tying the ends together. Belts receive more strain than other garments that we have discussed. In order to maintain the contour of a belt, it will be necessary to construct it for maximum strength. The outside foundation and the lining fabrics should be cut on the lengthwise grain of your fabric. This eliminates the fabric from distorting with wear. It may also be to your advantage to interface your fabrics before embellishing their surface. Use an iron-on interfacing

Belts for trimming strip pieced and a string of hearts designed by Author.

that can be pressed to the wrong sides of the belt and as well as the lining. Cut the iron-on interfacing without seam allowance. Press this material, following the manufacturers directions, on the wrong side of your fabrics within the seam lines. Eliminating this material from the seams will allow you to have a sharper and less bulky edge after the belt is reversed. If you do not wish to use iron-on interfacing, a layer of pellon fleece may give your belt the additional weight it may require. Experience will teach you which belt thickness you prefer.

You can line your belts, and reverse them in an inconspicuous area along a straight edge. Using a lining that slides easily may be a problem when you wear the belt. It can be annoying to continuously adjust your belt to the front with normal wear. Lining the belt in a contrasting cotton fabric can give you the advantage of having this accessory reversible. If you prefer, you may bind the belt edges with bias binding. This can offer a striking color element along the belt edge. Ribbons and accents shapes can be inserted into a belt before you line and reverse it. It would be great fun to stitch belt chatelaines for multible purposes. You can make a gardening belt to hang your tools upon, or a sewing belt with pin cushion, scissor holder or whatever. Your clothing projects are limited only by your imagination. Each project will suggest the next if you listen and are open to ideas. This is a magical experience. The more you do the more you will want to do. Naturally you will occasionally fail in your efforts, but failure is the best teacher of all. With experience your triumphs will be more frequent as a craftsman grows from each effort.

Index

Color Photo Index

Bibliography

Beyer, Jinny. *The Quilter's Album of Blocks and Borders.* Virginia, EPM Publications, Inc., 1980.

Hopkins, Mary Ellen. *It's Okay If You Sit On My Quilt.* Georgia, Yours Truly Publications, Inc. 1982.

Johnson, Mary Elizabeth. *Pillows.* Alabama, Oxmoor House Inc., 1978.

Schlotzhauer, Joyce. *The Curved Two-Patch System.* Virginia, EPM Publications, Inc., 1982.

Antique Coats and Clarks Thread Cabinet and small sewing tools owned by Author.

Other Books Published By AQS

Original Quilting Designs by Loraine Neff .... $ 7.95

America's Pictorial Quilts by Caron Mosey $19.95

Award Winning Applique Technique by Carolyn and Wilma Johnson $17.95

Thimbles and Accessories, Antique and Collectible by Averil Mathis $19.95

Missouri Heritage Quilts by Bettina Havig $14.95

Quilt Art Annual Engagement Calendar by AQS .... $ 8.95

Texas Quilts, Texas Treasures by Texas Heritage Quilt Society $24.95

Somewhere In Between: Quilts and Quilters of Illinois by Rita Barrow Barber $14.95

Scarlet Ribbons, American Indian Technique For Today's Quilters by Helen Kelley $15.95

Dear Helen, Can You Tell Me? . . . all about quilting designs by Helen Squire $12.95

Sets & Borders by Gwen Marston & Joe Cunningham $14.95

Irish Chain Quilts by Joyce B. Peaden $14.95

American Beauties: Rose & Tulip Quilts by Gwen Marston & Joe Cunningham $14.95

Collecting Quilts: Investments in America's Heritage by Cathy Florence $19.95

Add $1.00 additional for postage & handling.

American Quilter's Society

P.O. Box 3290 • Paducah, Kentucky 42001